Alfred Adler's

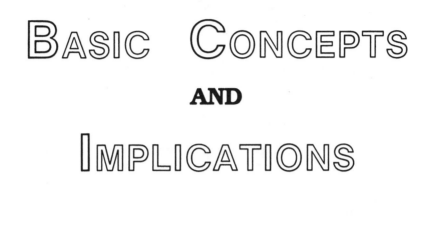

BASIC CONCEPTS

AND

IMPLICATIONS

Robert W. Lundin, Ph.D.
Kenan Professor of Psychology
The University of the South
Sewanee, Tennessee

Accelerated Development
A member of the Taylor & Francis Group

Alfred Adler's

Basic Concepts and Implications

Technical Development: Tanya Dalton
                         Sandra Gilmore
                         Marguerite Mader
                         Sheila Sheward

Library of Congress Cataloging-in-Publication Data

Lundin, Robert W. (Robert William), 1920-
Alfred Adler's basic concepts and implications.

Bibliography:p.
Includes index.
1. Personality. 2. Adler, Alfred, 1870-1937.
I. Title
BF698.L82 1989   150.19'53   88-71464
ISBN 0-915202-83-2

LCN: 88-71464

For information and ordering, contact:
Accelerated Development
A member of the Taylor & Francis Group
47 Runway Road, Suite G
Levittown, PA 19057-4700
1-800-821-8312

PREFACE

I have been teaching college students in the areas of personality and personality theory for better than three decades. During the course of these years, many books on personality theories have passed my desk. Almost all of them have contained chapters on Alfred Adler's psychology. In many cases the discussions have been incomplete. Furthermore, to my knowledge, no concise treatment of Adler's psychology exits today. My purpose in writing this book has been to present the basic principles of Adler's psychology in a form easily understood by students of psychology as well as a wider population interested in psychology.

Adler is one of the most important personality theories of the twentieth century. His ideas are as pertinent today as they were in the earlier part of this century when he first wrote them. Today, we live in a "high tech," "get ahead" world. Adler saw clearly the nature of human strivings and future goals. You need go no further than a corporate executive training program or a pricey self understanding seminar to hear the language of Adler's psychology. He wrote of needing to create personal goals, strivings for self enhancement and social interest, overcoming inferiorities, and developing a productive style of life. His ideas are pragmatic and present an optimistic attitude towards human nature. Likewise, he was a great proponent of the equality of the sexes.

This book is written for the intelligent layman as well as students of psychology and professionals engaged in the healing sciences. It is intended to improve our understanding of ourselves as well as others about us—those with whom we live, work, play, and in other ways interact. This general approach is reflected in the title of one of Alder's books, *Understanding Human Nature.*

His psychology continues to grow in popularity. Evidence for his popularity is to be found in many Institutes for Adlerian Psychology which exist all over the western world. Also many seminars are devoted to more short time study of Adler's theories. Although this is not a "how to improve your personality" book, an understanding of the concepts and implications presented can lead to greater self understanding. Adler believed very strongly that we all have the power to change our ways in order to develop a more satisfactory style of life.

Robert W. Lundin
Sewanee, Tennessee

CONTENTS

CHAPTER I

ALFRED ADLER AND INDIVIDUAL PSYCHOLOGY

Alfred Adler was born on February 7, 1870 in Rudolfschein, Austria, a suburb of Vienna, the son of a middle class grain merchant. Being the second born of eight children, he grew up in the shadow of a talented older brother. At the time, Vienna was one of the most important cultural centers of Europe known not only for its music (Mozart, the Strausses, Mahler) but for its art and science as well. Vienna was a mixture of gaiety and serious endeavors.

As a young child, Adler was very frail and delicate, suffering from rickets and attacks of glotis. At the age of three, one of his brothers died in the same bedroom in which he was sleeping. A year later Adler suffered a severe bout with pneumonia. At about the same time, he recalls visiting a doctor who said to his father, "Your child is lost" (Orgler, 1963, p. 2). At this point, he decided that he would become a doctor, a good doctor, not a bad one like the doctor who had talked so disparagingly to his father. Furthermore, in his early childhood, Adler had twice been hit by a carriage thus enhancing a fear of death which had begun with the earlier struggle with pneumonia. As a result of his weakness, his parents tended to pamper him. In a letter to Orgler he wrote: "During my first two years my mother pampered me, but when my younger brother was born she transferred her attention to him, and I felt dethroned and turned to my father whose favorite I was" (Orgler, 1963, p. 2).

His father's attitude of never taking anything for granted but finding out everything for himself made a lasting impression on him (Orgler, 1963).

At age five Adler started school. His rickets made him clumsy, particularly in sports. He was not a particularly good student in school and had to repeat mathematics in secondary school. By this time, one of his teachers advised his father to take him out of school to become an apprentice to a shoemaker. Fortunately, his father did not take the advice and so Adler intensified his academic efforts and eventually passed the mathematics course.

In secondary school, he had a particular interest in philosophy, psychology, political science, and sociology. His dream to become a physician went back to the early years and in 1888 he entered the medical school of the University of Vienna receiving his medical degree in 1895.

Even as a school boy Adler had been interested in social problems. This concern continued during his years in medical school. He enjoyed helping others with their school work. This strong concern for others had an important effect on his later thinking and theorizing as a social analyst. It is rather ironic that while in medical school he never attended any of the lectures on hysteria which were given by a then rather unknown physician by the name of Sigmund Freud. Adler never received any academic honors during his medical career. After his internship at the Viennese Hospital and Policlinic, he began his medical practice specializing in diseases of the eye. Here he first observed that people with poor eyesight frequently developed extremely sharp hearing. This observation was to be incorporated into one of his earliest writings, *Organ Inferiority and Its Psychical Compensations* (1917). From specializing in the eye, Adler turned his attention to the general practice of medicine and eventually to neurology and psychiatry.

During his early medical career he continued his interest in sociology and social problems. He enjoyed social gatherings and being with people. In 1897 he married Raissa Epstein, a very brilliant woman and an ardent Socialist.

In 1902 Adler first became acquainted with Freud. He never considered himself Freud's pupil, never attended any lectures on hysteria, and never was psychoanalyzed, a condition required of all psychoanalytic practitioners. Rather, Adler considered himself an associate and did join Freud's Wednesday night discussion groups as well as the Vienna Psychoanalytic Society. Adler's first association with Freud arose out of his defense of Freud's theory of dreams (Freud, 1900) which had been published two years earlier in 1900 and which was being vehemently attacked by the press.

Adler never considered himself a Freudian even though he was one of the earliest members of the inner circle. The two of them never developed a warm, interpersonal relationship. Adler never was the kind of person who would worship at the feet of his master.

Gradually, Adler's ideas became divergent from those of Freud. The differences between them were both theoretical and personal. In 1911, these differences came to a head when Adler was president of the Vienna Psychoanalytic Society. As president he was asked to present his views on psychoanalysis before the group. In a series of three papers, he expressed his strong opposition to Freud's sexual proclamations. What became clear was that these differences were irreconcilable. Accordingly, Adler resigned his presidency and, along with seven other members, left the group to form their own circle calling themselves *The Society for Free Psychoanalysis*. Adler also had been on the editorial staff of Freud's journal, *Zeitschrift fur psychoanalyse* and resigned that position. In 1912, the new group changed its name to the *Society for Individual Psychology*.

Rather soon afterwards a strong antithesis developed between Freud's and Adler's groups. Freud blamed Adler for his ambitious and obstinate ways. He called Adler a heretic and a plagiarist. In retrospect most writers agree that the strong personality differences accounted for a lot of the trouble. But strong theoretical differences existed as well.

1. Adler opposed Freud's strong emphasis on sex in his libido theory.

2. Adler considered the human personality as an indivisible unit, each person being a unique individual. Freud preferred certain separations as between consciousness and unconsciousness, and later on the division of the mental apparatus into the ego, super ego, and id.

3. Freud, in turn, criticized Adler's ego theory with its strong emphasis on consciousness and the functioning of the conscious ego in favor of an emphasis on the unconscious mind which was of utmost importance to Freud.

4. Adler opposed the penis envy as part of the Oedipus complex in favor of his own concept of the masculine protest (see Ch. 2; see also Mosak, 1979).

Following his departure from the Freudian circle, Adler published actively during the succeeding years. The following are some of his more important publications. The years indicated are of the first publication in German.

The Neurotic Constitution (1912)

The Practice of Individual Psychology (1920)

The Science of Living (1927)

Understanding Human Nature (1927)

The Problem of Neurosis (1929)

The Problem Child (1930)

What Life Should Mean To You (1931)

Social Interest (1933)

Clearly his most significant works appeared between the years 1920-1933.

In 1915, Adler suffered a setback when he was denied a teaching appointment at the University of Vienna. During World War I, he did psychiatric work with the Viennese Army. The years following World War I were difficult ones for Adler and the Austrian people in general. Much poverty, famine, and many epidemics were common. Ewen (1985) has suggested that these trying times contributed to Adler's socialistic feelings, although he refused to become involved in any of the political activities of the socialists.

During the 1920s, Adler turned his attention to children and education. In 1922, he founded what was probably the first child guidance clinic. Others followed in many of the public schools. The clinics were run by psychologists who served without pay. By 1934, Adler had established 28 such clinics.

In the early 1930s, Adler foresaw the development of Nazism. He had been born into the Jewish faith, but in 1904 had been converted to Christianity. In any event, in 1934 he moved to the United States where he taught at Long Island College of Medicine. In 1939, he died of a heart attack in Aberdeen, Scotland while on a lecture tour. He had had a heart condition of many years standing.

Unfortunately, no standard edition of Adler's complete works has been compiled as exists for the works of Freud and Jung. Probably his most important books number a dozen, although he also wrote many articles and monographs.

Adler's Psychology Today

When Adler came to the United States, the importance of his theories was not fully appreciated. As time progressed, Adler's psychology has assumed increasing popularity. In 1952, the *American Society for Adlerian Psychology* was founded. Two major journals are devoted to his psychology. *The Journal of Individual Psychology* and *The Individual Psychologist.* The *International Association for Individual Psychology* also publishes a *Newsletter.*

Many training centers offer certificates in Adlerian psychotherapy, counseling, and child guidance. In the United

States, they are located in New York, Chicago, Minneapolis, Berkeley, St. Louis, Dayton, Toledo, and Cleveland, and in Canada in Vancouver and Toronto. Furthermore, programs for the study of Individual Psychology are at several Universities including Oregon, West Virginia, Vermont, DePaul and Rhode Island.

Today Adlerian psychology has never been more popular. Considered earlier as superficial and applicable only to children, today it is regarded as a pioneering attempt to present a view of man that is practical, holistic, social, and teleological. Adlerian concepts are widely used, although frequently they are applied without proper credit to him. A few might be mentioned here and will be elaborated in greater detail in later chapters: (1) feelings of inferiority, (2) compensation, (3) strivings for superiority and self esteem, (4) future goal orientation, (5) style of life, (6) unity of the personality, (7) creative self, (8) order of birth, (9) achievement strivings, and (10) social interest.

The popularity of Adlerian psychology is not limited to the United States and Canada. Groups of people—psychiatrists, psychologists, counselors, and social workers—are devoted to the study of Individual Psychology in practically every country in Europe, including the cities of Vienna, Copenhagen, Stockholm, Paris, London, Brussels, Prague, Munich, and Berlin.

Adlerian theories also have had a marked influence on other contemporary approaches to psychology.

1. **Gestalt Psychology** has emphasized a holistic approach to many aspects of psychological activity such as perception, learning, memory, problem solving in favor of a reductionism of psychological processes to mechanistic elements.

2. **Existential Psychology** has taken a phenomenological approach (as did Adler) to the nature of man. It shares with Adler the basic assumption that man lives in interaction with the world, that man is future oriented, that problems of life arise from a freedom to choose one's goals and projects, and that man is concerned with the meaning of life (Ansbacher, 1977).

3. **Humanistic Psychology** as led by Abraham Maslow and Carl Rogers has set forth the premise that it is a "third force" in psychology today in opposition to traditional Freudian psychoanalysis and behaviorism as set forth by the experimental learning theorists, in particular, B.F. Skinner. Maslow considered the Adlerians as part of this third force with its emphasis on the creative power of man, and an anti-mechanistic approach to him. Teleology rather than causation is important and a holistic rather than an elementalistic approach should be followed besides an emphasis on man's subjectivity (Ansbacher, 1977).

EARLIER INFLUENCES ON ADLER'S PSYCHOLOGY

In the history of philosophy and science, men have set forth new ideas which are bound to be influenced by those who came before. Adler is no exception.

Sigmund Freud

Adler considered Freud's influence on him to be mostly negative. Yet, it must be remembered that his association with Freud lasted about ten years. Probably, the most important influence of Freud was the concept that the human personality is driven by dynamic strivings. Although they differed on the exact nature of the striving, the emphasis on motivational forces can not be denied. In his early writings, Freud stressed the sexual libido and later the life and death instincts as the source of all psychic energy. Adler stressed a striving for power in his early writings and later a striving for superiority and self-esteem.

Carl Marx

Early in his career, Adler became acquainted with the Socialism of Marx, not so much as it applied to politics and economics but in the matter of social equality and the strivings to overcome inferiority. In his concept of the masculine protest, Adler was constantly concerned with the existing attitude of inequality between man and woman. He advocated an attitude of equality for both sexes which shows a relationship to Marx's stress on a greater equality for the lower classes.

Fredrich Nietzche

Nietzsche had altered Schopehnauer's idea of the will to live to a will for power, and the rewards of the successful should not be considered evil or false. The will to power is natural in man as it is expressed as a striving to overcome and be mighty. Adler's striving from the inferior to the superior was most likely inspired by Nietzsche's principle. A will to power in Nietzsche's conception is the right of the strong to dominate. Adler's early interpretation of the striving as being one for power reflects Nietzche's thinking.

Hans Vaihinger

Adler had read Vaihinger's book, *The Philosophy of "As If"* in 1911 in which he stated that many of the ideals and concepts we live by are not really true to our own experience, let alone valid beyond experience. In fact, they turn out to be fictions or falsifications of our real experience, but we use these fictions for our own convenience and edification. These fictions appear to be more pleasant and profitable than an acceptance of the facts of experience as they really are. Adler accepted, at least in part, what Vaihinger was saying and added to it the notion of future strivings. Thus, in "fictional finalism" the final goals we strive for may be mere fictions, all of which is not necessarily bad.

Henri Bergson

Bergson was one of the most important French pragmatists of the nineteenth century. He stressed the usefulness of experience and the utility of memories of our immediate experience. Thus, these memories help us to anticipate the future. Likewise, everyday experience tends to be forward looking. Here we encounter a teleology or notion of future strivings affecting our present behavior.

From Bergson, Adler also encountered the concept of *elan vital* or the thrusting or pushing or flinging ourselves forward.

Man has a vital urge. For Adler, whatever name one might call this urge was not the real issue. Whether it be called power, superiority, striving for self enhancement, there was always a push and that was what was important.

With this brief review of Adler's life and contributions, the prior influences on his thinking, primarily from nineteenth century philosophy and his place in psychology today, we are ready to begin with one of his earliest tenets, inferiority and its compensations.

CHAPTER II

INFERIORITY AND COMPENSATION

Many of Adler's early writings had to do with feelings of inferiority and the ways we compensate or make up for them. At the time, around 1907, he was still associated with Freud and the idea of compensation, particularly for organ inferiority, seemed reasonably compatible with the Freudian notion of displacement. In displacement, the satisfaction of a frustrated instinct could be at least partially fulfilled by finding a substitute object as illustrated in the case of a sexually frustrated male who seeks satisfaction by attending X-rated movies or reading sexy novels.

ORGAN INFERIORITY

As a medical practitioner, Adler was concerned with treating diseases. As he put it, disease tends to attack inferior organs. Inferior organs were identified as those body parts which were inhibited in their growth or altered in whole or in part. The causes of organ inferiority might be genetic or the result of some environmental damage, accident, or disease. In his reference to inferior organs, he included the sense organs as well as various systems of the body including the digestive, respiratory, genito-urinary, muscular, and the central nervous system including the brain.

Adler first studied the problem of organ inferiority in an early monograph entitled, *A Study of Organ Inferiority and Its Psychical Compensations* (1917). Not only did inferior organs lend themselves more susceptible to disease, but they also could influence psychic (psychological) experiences. For example, he observed that children's misbehavior might be attributed to organ inferiority, but also could be attributed to an unsuccessful compensation. Of course, an organ inferiority does not necessarily lead to a bad effect. The compensation could take the form of a very desirable pattern of reactions. Adler observed further that a disease of the heart could strengthen heart muscles so the malfunction could be overcome. When a diseased kidney is removed, the remaining kidney becomes enlarged thus compensating for the loss of the diseased one.

Even more important the compensation could take the place in a psychological way. In this instance, he cited the example of Demosthenes who was a stutterer and overcame the difficulty by placing little pebbles in his mouth while practicing his speech and became one of the greatest orators of ancient Greece. Or one could cite the case of Teddy Roosevelt who as a child was a weakling, but compensated by being a superior horseman and joining the "rough riders." Adler also cited famous painters who had eye difficulties. Likewise, inferior vision could frequently stimulate the imagination as in cases of writers with poor eyesight who could make their readers "see" things through their magnificent verbal descriptions. The expression "blind seers" illustrates this compensation. Homer was supposed to have been blind and Milton wrote some of his most beautiful work during his blindness. The same holds true for an inferior sense of hearing. Beethoven wrote his greatest music when he was totally deaf as did the Czech composer Smetana. Helen Keller, who was rendered both deaf and blind at an early age, graduated from Radcliff, wrote her own life story, and learned about the world through her sense of touch.

Sometimes one sense organ could compensate for the inferiority of another. Adler observed that people with poor eyesight typically developed a more acute sense of hearing. Musicians frequently had eye difficulties including blindness. An elderly lady with both failing eyesight and hearing developed an acute sense of smell whereby she could smell smoke a half mile away.

Adler also applied his theory to people who were left handed and to men who were short in stature. He observed that left handed children with proper training could acquire superior handwriting skills and become good sketchers. Men who were small in stature might become extremely skillful or witty or become great leaders, like Napoleon Bonaparte. Of course, the compensation might not always be positive. Short men sometimes become extremely arrogant and domineering or despots and tyrants.

Adler emphasized that the organ inferiority itself was not the significant factor but rather was the *attitude* one takes toward the problem. If the attitude was positive, the results would show themselves in a favorable compensation. If the attitude was one of helplessness, the inferiority might influence one's entire attitude towards life leading to exaggerated feelings of inferiority or the *Inferiority Complex* (see the next section of this chapter). Organ inferiorities could have other harmful effects psychologically which could lead eventually to a variety of maladjustments and mental disorders. Later Adler wrote of the inferior style of life which resulted from unfortunate compensations for organ inferiority.

GENERALIZED OR UNIVERSAL FEELINGS OF INFERIORITY

Organ inferiority was not the only cause of inferiority feelings. Adler believed inferiority feelings were universal in humans.

To "be a human being means the possession of a feeling of inferiority that is constantly pressing on towards its own conquest" (Adler, 1938, p. 73). Adler was reflecting Darwin when he stated that the fundamental law in life was that of overcoming deficiencies and inadequacies. Life itself becomes a struggle of adaptation to the demands of the world. The demands and problems posed by living in the external world are often greater than man's ability to cope with them. Thus, feelings of inferiority arise out of our inability to deal with the external environment. In extreme cases all kinds of physical, emotional, and mental disturbances may result.

Still, Adler's attitude toward mankind and his environment was optimistic. In his book, *Social Interest*, he wrote:

Who can seriously doubt that the human individual treated by nature in such a step-motherly fashion has been provided with the blessing of a strong feeling of inferiority and that urges him towards a plus situation, towards security and conquest? And this tremendous feeling of inferiority is awakened afresh and repeated in every infant and little child as the fundamental fact of human development. (1938, p. 89)

Thus, the natural feelings of inferiority arise out of the infant's smallness and helplessness, in difficulties he or she faces in the life situation. The child realizes at an early age that bigger people are able to satisfy their needs more completely, to better prepare them for life. It is said that the little toddler lives in a world of big legs: legs of people, chairs, and tables. Some children will attempt to model adults directly in order to satisfy their own needs. Others will accept their own weakness and helplessness. In either case, feelings of inferiority, inadequacy, and uncertainty arise which give rise to a need, sooner or later, to compensate for the difficulties in the environment. Every child is faced with innumerable obstacles in life. In fact, Adler wrote, "Every voluntary act begins with a feeling of inadequacy" (1927, p. 38).

Clearly, then, the tendency to compensate is not limited to making up for bodily deficiencies. Infants enter the world as the weakest things in their surroundings. Body movements are uncoordinated and undeveloped. The earliest means for making their desires known are primarily limited to crying. Little children are completely dependent on those around them for the maintenance of their existence. The impressions of the world are tied up with a feeling of weakness and insecurity. In the first years of life, the child begins to master the environment and models those in the surroundings. Coupled with this weakness are going to be minor organ inferiorities, such as childhood illnesses and accidents. Later, during the school years, rivalries, hostilities, and disappointments occur.

Adler placed great emphasis on the order of birth as affecting the personality of a child. The first born is the "dethroned king," being abandoned in part by the birth of the second. The middle child is constantly trying to catch up with an older brother or sister, but never really does, at least, in the early years. The second child is always behind. The last born may be in a more desirable position, but also might be the product of aging parents, only to be spoiled or pampered. Adler considered *pampering* and *neglect* to be major factors leading to a faulty style of life.

Another problem also exists with children of the female sex. In many societies, boys are preferred. Recent studies (Stark, 1985) have shown that a majority of parents would like their first born to be a boy, and fathers overwhelmingly admit that if he shall have only one child it should be a boy. Although Adler considered the sexes to be equal psychologically, he frequently equated femininity with weakness and masculinity with strength. (See later section on the masculine protest.) By and large, because of these attitudes, girls are more likely to feel inferior. The boy is the one who carries on the family name, who inherits the title to become the king or duke.

Unfortunate patterns of upbringing may foster further inferiority, a child may be rejected or unwanted, he or she may not be the favorite, mothers may be domineering, fathers may be neglecting. All of these factors in the child's upbringing and natural weakness will lead to universal feelings of inferiority. For the most part this is not particularly abnormal. It is a part of living and growing up. Each step on the way to adulthood will have its compensations. Often the compensations derive simply out of the process of growth. As the children grow older they are able to master tasks they could not undertake at an earlier age.

Adler summed the problem up in this way:

> . . . inferiority feelings are not in themselves abnormal. They are the cause of all improvements in the position of mankind. Science itself, for example, can arise only when people feel their ignorance and their need to further the future . . . Indeed, it seems to be that all our human culture is based upon feelings of inferiority . . . men are the weakest of all creatures." (Adler, 1931, pp. 55-56)

EXAMPLES OF SPECIFIC COMPENSATIONS

In a general way, feelings of inferiority serve as an impetus for the strivings for superiority (see Ch. 4). These strivings become the basic dynamic force in all human personalities. The specific ways in which we compensate for inferiority constitutes one of the factors that determines our style of life.

In the earlier section on organ inferiority was mentioned a number of ways in which people compensate for their organ inferiorities. A fat girl develops a bubbly personality. The golfer deprived of one arm becomes a master player and so on. As already indicated, however, in many cases, the source of the inferiority comes from the environment, the family situation, or position in the birth order. In the following instances, a particular compensation could very much dominate a person's entire style of life. In other instances, the compensation may only be a temporary one. Here are some typical specific examples.

A college girl, deprived of the attention of men, throws herself into her academic pursuits to become a straight A student.

A maiden lady, never offered a proposal of marriage, becomes a kindergarten teacher taking care, in part, of other people's children.

A student, seemingly unable to make good grades, becomes a star footbal player.

A boy, inept in playing athletics in college, becomes a superior pianist.

A man, who came from and impoverished financial background, becomes a millionaire.

A child, who was a social misfit, grows up to be a famous actor.

A girl, belonging to a racial minority group, becomes a popular leader of the majority cause.

A man, frustrated by his employment situation, compensates by spoiling his children.

An only child, wishing to have other brothers and sisters, begets eight children after he is married.

A girl, reared in the lap of luxury, grows up to become a leader of an anti-establishment movement.

A housewife, deprived of a college education, marries a college professor.

With regard to compensation, Adler cited the Cinderella fairy tale. Here the slighted and ill-treated Cinderella, mistreated by her evil step-mother and selfish step-sisters, overcame her inferiority with the help of her fairy god mother, finds her Prince Charming and lives happily ever after. However, Adler also warns us about people with strong inferiority feelings who may overindulge in too many unrealistic fantasies of success which in no way solve the problems and which may eventually result in a variety of psychological disorders.

INFERIORITY AND SUPERIORITY COMPLEXES

In some cases the normal inferiority feelings become highly exaggerated to dominate an individual's style of life. Here Adler applied the term, *inferiority complex*. The difference between the normal feelings of inferiority and the inferiority complex is merely a matter of degree and not kind. These exaggerated feelings will lead to a variety of undesirable personality traits such as shyness, cowardice, an increased need for support, submissive obedience, and masochistic tendencies along with some compensatory tendencies such as impudence, impulsiveness, stubbornness, defiance or sadistic impulses, all of which culminate in an exaggerated feeling of being slighted. Thoughts of revenge become directed against the self and the environment. The child with an inferiority complex looks for the possibility of evading difficulties instead of trying to overcome them.

Adler stated: "Imagine the goal of the child who is not confident of being able to solve his problems: How dismal the world must appear to such a child: Here we find timidity, introspectiveness, distrust and all those other characteristics and traits with which the weakling seeks to defend himself" (1927, p. 33).

The inferiority complex is one of the main contributory factors to neurotic behavior. In many places, Adler stated the two conditions typical of all neuroses, the *inferiority complex* and a *lack of social interest* (see Ch. 4). The neurotic is incapable of coping with the inevitable problems of life and so results in what Adler called "cheap tricks." These include evading responsibility, trying the easy way out, placing unrealistic demands on others, blaming one's shortcomings on others, seeking revenge, being over sensitive, having exaggerated feelings of guilt or any other strategy which might put one's tremendous inferiority feelings to their own advantage.

On the other hand, the *superiority complex* is likewise a neurotic technique of disguising the intolerable inferiority complex. This embodies a false belief (even a delusion) that one is better or above other people. The superiority complex should not be confused with normal strivings for superiority as the basic dynamic force in all personality development (see Ch. 4). In contrast to useful strivings for superiority, the superiority complex is another "cheap trick" as an attempt to overcome the strong feelings of inferiority.

Adler described the superiority complex as a character trait or attitude an individual has of his or her own super human gifts and accomplishments. It can manifest itself in exaggerated demands an individual places on him or herself or others. It can be expressed as vanity towards one's personal appearance, outlandish patterns of dressing such as a masculine appearance in women and a feminine appearance in men.

With regard to personality traits, the individual may be arrogant, snobbish, snooty, bossy, domineering or express a tendency to run other people's lives, or a desire to attach oneself to prominent and important people. It can be an attempt to rule those who are weaker, or of an inferior status, or an intentional deception. These people give the impression of utter conceit. They are regarded as "stuck on themselves." They will brag excessively, exaggerate their accomplishments. They insist on being the center of attention. They show strong enthusiasm for unimportant matters. In a conversation, they will direct the talk to themselves. In their egocentricity, they are unable to establish good personal relationships with others. Often they express an intense striving for power without regard for the feelings of others. This might eventually end up in criminal behavior.

The superiority complex, then, is a mask, an undesirable compensation for inferiority. Most people who are really superior usually will show some sense of modesty, even though they are inwardly aware of their accomplishments. In a sense, no *true* superiority complex, as such, exists. The behavior is merely a cover up for the deep-seated feelings of inferiority. Ordinarily, it can be easily spotted for its exaggerated manifestations.

MASCULINE PROTEST

Some writers have misunderstood Adler's conception of the *masculine protest.* Of the two interpretations, many mention only one, which is the later interpretation.

The first and earliest interpretation had to do with Adler's conception of drive or the basic motivational force in man. This interpretation of drive was at variance with that of Freud's. At the time around 1910, Freud was stressing the importance of the sexual libido, whereas Adler referred to the main dynamic principle as the *masculine protest.* This was first interpreted as a striving to be strong and powerful. According to Ansbacher and Ansbacher, "Masculine protest is interpreted as a striving to be strong and powerful as a compensation for the feeling of inferiority" (1956, p. 45).

In this context, masculinity and femininity stand for strength and weakness. As it turned out, this choice of a metaphor did not appear to be a satisfactory one.

By 1930, Adler had finalized his concept of the dynamic strivings as a striving for superiority and perfection. He limited the term "masculine protest" to a new and more restricted meaning. Although this second interpretation is usually applied to women, it also can apply to men as well. For women, it becomes a protest against their feminine role in our society.

Attitudes toward the woman's role in European and American society fifty years ago were much different from what they are today. Men were referred to as the "stronger sex" and women, the "weaker sex". So the weakness of women became associated with inferiority. If we look into history, there is an obvious preference for the male. The lineage of royalty is passed on to the males. Parents often continue to propagate offspring until a boy is born, in part to carry on the family name or title. One of the worst insults you could tell a boy is that he is acting like a girl. As women depended on men for help and support, a feeling of inferiority arose. Freud, for example, firmly believed that "woman's place was in the home." Not until 1920 did women win the right to vote. Woman's place was to bear children and take care of the household.

Even though Adler considered men physically stronger, which is still true today, he nonetheless considered them equal psychologically. This being the case despite a general discrimination against women in the work force, the masculine protest could be considered a positive compensation.

In most of Adler's writings, he placed great emphasis on the role of the home environment, the family constellation, the order of birth as significant social forces contributing to personality development. Unlike later social analysts such as Karen Horney and Erich Fromm, he tended to ignore the significance of attitudes and behaviors of society and culture in general. However, attitudes of society toward women's role turned to be the *exception*. In this instance, he emphasized society's rule.

Beginning in the 1930s, women began to protest the notion of female inferiority. Some little girls preferred to dress like boys, play "boys' games" or prefer to be called by a boy's name. As time progressed, women gained greater rights and began to enter vocations and professions usually limited to men. World War II had a lot to do with with this change in attitude because of an absence of men in the work force to do factory work, enforce the law, drive taxis, and so on. Certain professions such as the law, medicine, banking, engineering, and architecture began to accept women. The whole equal rights movement is striking evidence of the success of the masculine protest. Surely, if Adler were alive today, he would be pleased with the progress of women and the validity of the masculine protest concept.

Although the concept of the masculine protest is usually applied to women, it also can apply to men and boys as well. Take the case of a boy who has grown up in a matriarchal family. He might rebel against the domination of the mother and take on a more exaggerated female role. He might become the cook of the house, or be a hairdresser or designer of women's clothing. Another possibility would be that he was not able to fulfill the masculine role expected of him, thus assuming more feminine patterns of behavior.

Masculine protest, then, is another form of compensation. In many instances where the law now prohibits the discrimination against women in instances of job opportunities and pay, it has had positive effects. Remember, however, that when Adler was writing about the masculine protest, men were usually given preferred status. Of course, the matter is still not completely solved. Women still tend to take on their husband's name when they marry even though no law requires it. Women are still more likely to care for the children, do the housework, and cook the meals. People may still find it unusual to encounter a male nurse or telephone operator.

Also negative aspects exist regarding the masculine protest. Some women may so overcompensate that the masculine protest takes the form of a superiority complex which serves as a foundation for pathological behavior including crime and the neuroses. She might completely reject her sexual role as a woman and a partner to the male in sexual intercourse.

Just as compensation has its counterpart in the Freudian theory of displacement, the masculine protest also has its analogy in Freud's concept of *penis envy,* a part of the Oedipus Complex in little girls. In penis envy, the little girl feels deprived of the sex organ her father has and blames her mother for bringing her into the world without it. Although Adler did not place the emphasis on the sex drive as did Freud, the fact of the masculine protest can be interpreted as a desire on the part of a girl or woman to have the power, strength, and rights typically attributed to men. In conclusion, the statement should be reiterated that Adler completely rejected the stereotype of male dominance and considered women to be equals to men.

The concepts of inferiority and compensations are two of the cornerstones of Adlerian theory. They have their positive and negative aspects. Without feelings of inferiority, many people would never strive to overcome and never accomplish what they are capable of doing. Compensations constitute part of the style of life. Excessive inferiority and poor compensations can likewise lead the individual into many kinds of psychological difficulty. The ideas of inferiority as something to be overcome sets the stage for goals towards which an individual strives, which is the subject of the next chapter.

IMPLICATIONS

Alder made clear that inferiority feelings were not necessarily abnormal. In addressing the basic concepts of inferiority and compensation, a bit of objective analysis can be useful. We first ask ourselves, are a person's feelings the result of some biological defect or are they the result of environmental circumstances? If a biological defect, is it correctable? Or, if environmental circumstances were the causes in the person's upbringing which have lead to the inferiority feelings? If so, these environmental factors might include domineering parents, being unfairly compared with a brother or sister, inconsistent discipline, favoritism, or excessive demands placed on the person.

One of the most basic means of coping with inferiority is compensation. This technique may help a person adjust to life's problems or it can make them even worse. The compensation may lead to better adaptation or may lead to greater maladjustment.

A case in point of poor compensation is that of a young man who was reared in an authoritarian home. As a child he was not allowed to play with children of religious denominations other than his. He became a lonely child with few friends. As a result, his interpersonal relationships suffered, particularly with members of his own sex. At work he gave the impression that he knew more than his superiors and was excessively demanding of those who worked under his supervision. Instead of engaging in competitive sports (golf, tennis, handball), he took to a ritual of individual jogging and working out in the gym by himself. Here, his only competition was himself. He did not have to suffer the inferiority of losing to others.

When he conversed with others, he gave the impression of being the ultimate authority on many things: art, music, travel, automobiles, or any subject about which he had some knowledge. This man was suffering from a superiority (compensation) complex which expressed itself as a mask for his intense underlying feelings of inferiority.

FICTIONALISM AND FINALISM

The next step in the evolution of Adler's system led to the development of *future goals* towards which we strive. Freud had considered the *goals in life* to be the objects which served to satisfy our instincts; food for hunger, a member of the opposite sex for the sex instinct, and so on. Early in his career, Adler had differed with Freud regarding both the goals and the nature of the striving forces. In this chapter, we shall consider the nature of the goals and how they are formulated. In the following chapter, we shall consider the nature of the striving forces.

UNITY OF THE PERSONALITY

One of Adler's earliest and most basic principles was the unity of the organism. Every human being is a single, indivisible person constituting a unity in itself. No psychological expression can be viewed in isolation but must be regarded in relation to the total personality. If a patient came to Adler with a particular complaint such as an inability to sleep at night, Adler would most likely not prescribe a sleeping pill for the insomnia but would attempt to relate this particular symptom to the entire personality structure.

In psychological theorizing this approach is described as *holistic*, or dealing with the whole. Each person is an individual and must be dealt with as such. One can now understand at this point why Adler called his approach, *Individual Psychology*. The holistic approach is in opposition to one which considers the human personality as made up of a series of elements or parts. For example, a trait theory of personality is ordinarily one which considers a person as being made up of a number of different behavior patterns, each of which may or may not be related to the others. Such a theory is also often referred to as an *omnibus theory.* The analogy here is that the contents of a bus consists of a number of separate people each one of which may be totally unrelated to another. In contrast, Adler considered each person to be a complete unity, one who was unique but still a complete human being.

The holistic approach is also anti-mechanistic. We can not consider an individual as made up of a lot of single parts, operating like a machine. Adler's approach stressed a vitalism rather than a mechanism. John Watson, the founder of Behaviorism, in 1913, took a very mechanistic approach to the nature of man. Here we have a person made up of a series of single reflexes. Adler's approach always attempted to study the whole organism and not be concerned with little bits of behavior. Life, for Adler, begins from one fertilized egg and all of the parts develop from this single cell (Ansbacher, 1977).

Unlike the Freudian conception of the human mental apparatus made up of three parts (ego, super ego, and id) and consisting of conflicting forces (usually unconscious), Adler considered the person as a dynamic unity. Regarding the conscious/unconscious dichotomy, Adler wrote, "The conscious and unconscious are not separate and conflicting parts, but complimentary and compensatory parts of one and the same reality" (1929a, p. 29).

The unity of the personality also must be considered on a time dimension. Each person's life is a single manifestation beginning in the past, going into the present, and finally directing itself toward the future. No gaps are in the lifespan. Throughout life a person encounters another person in thousands of different ways, but always the entire person, whether a friend, a relative, a coworker, or an associate with whom you deal.

FICTIONALISM

In 1911, a German philosopher, Hans Vaihinger published a book entitled *The Philosophy of "As If."* This occurred in the same year in which Adler broke with Freud and his followers. Adler read the book in its first German edition published in Berlin. The following year (1926), Adler published his own work, *The Neurotic Constitution,* considered by some to be his best. Parts of it reflect a strong influece of Vaihinger.

According to Vaihinger, we all live by a series of fictions which are ideas, usually conscious, which have no real counterpart in reality. Yet, as ideals, they have great practical value in our everyday lives. These fictions become working principles which we accept as a basis for our activities.

Vaihinger distinguished these fictions from hypotheses. Hypotheses, he said, can be put to the test and can either be verified or found to be false and thus discarded. If a fiction were put to the test, it would collapse because it lacked any real validity.

However, the fictions make life more pleasant and livable. For example, one is more convenient and agreeable by acting "as if " the universe was a completely orderly and convenient affair. According to Vaihinger, we create a fiction of natural laws "as if " all atoms moved in a completely orderly fashion. Likewise, for comfort one can believe in an all powerful God who is good, kind, and compassionate. This belief, in reality, simply does not apply to the way things really happen. If God loves and looks after us, how is it that so many miserable, poor, and unfortunate people are in the world? But we create the fiction that God is caring for all mankind.

Furthermore, for convenience one's fellow man can be viewed as if he were essentially good, although our experience does not really confirm that. On the other hand, we might *make believe* that the doctrine of "original sin" seems to account for man's failings.

Vaihinger went on to point out all objects in the world are subjected to the falsification of "as if." We regard them not as our experiences, nor in accordance with what is purely logical. We invent the fictions to conform to certain values and ideals that we have been taught. To say that, "All men are created equal" is a convenient and pleasant idea, particularly in a democracy. But if so, how do we account for the rare geniuses like Leonardo da Vinci, Beethoven, or Aristotle. And what about the poor mentally retarded whose intellectual functionings are so poor that they may not even be aware of their own existence? Another pleasant thought is to believe that "We will get our rewards in heaven," but nobody has been there and back to tell us so. The idea that "Good deeds will be rewarded on this earth and bad deeds punished" fits the same fiction. One might wish that all criminals will be caught and given their just due, but the real facts tell us that many criminals profit, get by the law, and are never taken to justice as long as they live.

When the real experiences and events do not fit our expectations, we can alter them in our minds so that they do fit. We may censor, leave out or alter what does not apply to our fictions. We ignore what is evil in the hero and what is good in the villain and then add a happy ending regardless of how absurd or contrary to the facts such an ending might be.

Fictions can be grouped into various categories, as the following examples will illustrate:

1. **Abstract:** the normal or average man as found in a statistical distribution. The fact is the absolutely average man does not exit.

2. **Symbolic:** fictions based on analogies. "He who pays the piper calls the tune."

3. **Heuristic:** a false discovery based on a false hypothesis.

4. **Practical:** "Man is free to think and do as he pleases." But are any of us really free?

The striking influence of Vaihinger on Adler was to give a philosophical framework for developing his subjective finalism (see next section). Adler considered that fictions could not be reduced to objective causes, but were mental structures, creations of the human mind. As we shall see, Adler combined the idea of fictions with his conception of the final goal which usually was also a fiction.

FINALISM AND TELEOLOGY

A teleological approach stresses future goals and purposes. It considers our strivings for the future as affecting our present behavior. This is in complete opposition to determinism which considers the present as a product of the past. Whereas, Freud was a complete determinist, Adler tended to stress teleology. He did not deny or ignore determinism entirely, but rather was simply a matter of which was more important.

For Adler, the goal of life became the governing principle or the final cause. The *source* of the striving energies is not what is important, rather what counts is the ultimate goal. Adler believed that a person would not know what to do with himself or herself if no orientation towards some goal exists. Our psychological processes of thinking, feeling, or any other act need to have some goal in mind.

He wrote: "The psychic life of man is determined by his goal . . . No human being can think, feel, will, dream, without all these activities being determined, continued, modified and directed towards an ever-present objective" (Adler, 1927, p. 29).

What is clear in the quote is that Adler was paying less attention to causation than to teleology. He does not completely deny determinism as it exists in infancy and childhood, but he stresses the goal seeking process which is developed very early in life. Frequently a child will overemphasize a scraped knee in order to gain the future goal of sympathy or an adult may depend on a headache to gain the attention and affection of a spouse.

Little children typically want to "look forward to something" whether it be a forthcoming birthday party next week, going to the movies this coming Friday, or a trip to the zoo in two weeks. Adler was saying that our future strivings guide our present lives.

All future strivings are directed toward some goal whether it be specific or all comprehensive.

> We have often found how people differ in their secret goals. The goal, although unknown to the individual, directs unobtrusively and unshakably all psychological expressive forms. When one knows the goal, one can comprehend his personality, because one knows its frame of reference to the tasks of life. (Adler 1956, p. 72)

At the beginning of this chapter, reference was made to Adler's conception of the unity of the personality. He wrote: "The final goal . . . unifies the personality and renders all behaviour comprehensible" (Adler 1956, p. 94).

The choice of the goal is neither the product of heredity nor environment, but the product of a free, creative choice and that choice is made early in life between the ages of four and five. Although the goal may not be directly perceived and incompletely understood, Adler believed that it determines the direction of a child's activity. For example, a young boy may imitate his father as a means of striving for success.

Although Adler did not make a clear distinction between consciousness and unconsciousness, the obscurity of the goal would indicate that in some instances the final goal may be operating at the unconscious level. In the meantime, since the final goal may only be vaguely known or not know at all, many more conscious subgoals can be created which are preliminary to the final one. In some way, however, they will tend to fit together in some consistent pattern. When the final goal is known, the subgoals take on a remarkable significance (Adler, 1956).

For example, a student decides to go to college. Here, college graduation is probably a subgoal. What about after college? His subgoal again can be that a college degree will give him or her greater opportunities for making a living. So, the next sub-goal may be finding a job with good opportunity for financial success. And so one climbs the financial ladder to an executive position, and so on. The final goal may be to become a multimillionaire, but one may never have been entirely conscious of the real nature of the final goal because it really was a fiction. After all, how many of us ever really become multimillionaires?

THE FICTIONAL FINAL GOAL

Just as the fictions are subjective, so is the final goal. Fictions are ideas of a positive nature. In the fiction was where Adler found the basis for his subjectivistic, finalistic psychology. Unlike Freud, Adler was optimistic about human nature. Freud took a rather dismal nature of the future of mankind. Adler's optimism is reflected in a finalism that would be acceptable, agreeable, and encouraging.

Thus, Adler combined the notion of the fiction with that of the final goal to become the fictional final goal, or "guiding fiction." In describing the goals and the future as fictional, Adler was expressing the idea of a subjective future. The future goal really exists in the present, but not necessarily in the present consciousness. Nevertheless, the goal is the super-ordinate guiding idea.

Nor can the origin of the goal be reduced to objective determinism. Adler does allow heredity, environment, organ inferiorities, and past experience to be of use in the mind's process of forming the future goal (Ansbacher & Ansbacher, 1956). The future goal still is of the individual's own making.

This finalism also implies that a person is usually unaware of his or her final goals. Ordinarily, Adler did not dwell on the nature of the unconscious as did Freud, but it is in this conception of the hidden nature of the final goal that we get close to Adler's conception of the unconscious.

The following points regarding the fictional final goal have been summarized by Ansbacher and Ansbacher (1956) as follows:

1. The principle of the fictional final goal represents the principle of internal, subjective causation of psychological events.

2. The goal is created by the individual but is largely unknown. Here, Adler believed that although the final goal is individually created by each person, it is not usually understood.

3. The goal also becomes the principle of unity of the personality. It becomes the basic governing principle by which the personality operates.

4. The goal also becomes the focus of a person's orientation to the real world.

5. Finally, the goal is one aspect of an individual's compensation for his or her inferiorities. It becomes a device by which an individual is able to pull himself or herself up by the bootstraps, so to speak. Actually, it serves two compensatory functions. First, it initiates a compensation and, secondly, it allows for positive feelings in the presence of which feelings of inferiority exist. The goal itself also might be a compensation. In Adler's case, his goal set early in life was to be a good physician. This goal became a compensation for his own frailty and poor health as a child. In this case, however, the goal seemed to be conscious rather than subjectively unconscious. Perhaps the unconscious fictional aspect was to be an eminent psychodynamic theorist, of which, certainly in his youth, he was unaware.

Having considered the nature of the goals towards which we strive, in the next chapter is considered the basic striving forces which give us the push to the achievement of these goals. Here the main strivings are for superiority and social interest.

IMPLICATIONS

Since Adler maintained a strong teleological approach to human personality, setting up future goals is important. These future strivings are evident in childhood. Children like to have something to look forward to: an upcoming party, next week's Little League game, or a promised treat. A child may be asked, what do you want to be when you grow up: a doctor, policeman, or firefighter? Even at this early age the goals may be fictions.

In the developmental process the future strivings can take the form of sub-goals; getting a high mark on a test, graduating from college, buying a new car. The long term goals will probably be more fictional. Yet, there is nothing wrong with asking ourselves what these fictions might be; to make a lot of money, to marry a beautiful woman or handsome man, to provide adequately for our retirement, to live happily ever after.

Adler maintained that it is perfectly healthy to have fictional goals. Furthermore, we may not even be aware of what they are. The problem with some people is that they have no goals at all, real or fictional. They are floundering about like a row boat on a rough sea. Since we all have inborn strivings, the procedure is to have these directed toward some ends.

CHAPTER **IV**

STRIVINGS FOR SUPERIORITY AND SOCIAL INTEREST

In the previous chapter was pointed out that Adler stressed as his first basic principle, the unity of the personality. To be consistent with this unity principle, he did not believe as Freud did, that each person has many different drives or instincts. Freud had divided the instincts into two classes, life and death. Adler's early conception was that confluence of drives exists where all drives merged, as in the branches of a stream, all of which merge into the main one. In 1908, he conceived of the idea of the "confluence of drives." At this time he was still in the Freudian camp. Freud had postulated a different physiological basis for each drive. Adler, on the other hand, suggested that rather than treating each drive separately, one ought to consider them as a confluence of energies merging into a single striving force. At this point, one needs to note that both Freud and Adler used the same German word (Trieb) which can be translated either as "drive" or "instinct." Also, at about this same time, Adler developed the notion of a "superordinated dynamic force" which would direct the confluence of the other drives. Thus, the separate drives lose their separate nature and subject themselves to a higher principle of motivation. At first to Adler this seemed to be a primary force that could be identified as an *aggressive* drive. For example, he observed in young children a certain hostility towards the environment. He also noted that the aggressive drive seemed to be pre-eminent in individuals who had organic inferiorities. In children, it could be expressed in its purest form in fighting, wrestling, biting, competition or some cruel activities. Little children often tend to be cruel towards their playmates until they eventually have learned otherwise. In adulthood, aggression is observed in competition and in extreme forms in criminal and revolutionary activities. Certain occupations tended to promote the drive: the judge, policeman, teacher, minister or politician. However, he also observed the cultural transformation of the aggressive drive. Here Adler pre-dates Freud. It was not until 1920 that Freud conceived of the death instinct from which aggression was a derivative and described it in *Beyond the Pleasure Principle* (1920). In 1910, Adler substituted the term "masculine protest." In its first interpretation, he equated it with the aggressive striving for masculinity or strength or force as opposed to femininity as equated with weakness (see Ch. 2).

STRIVING FOR POWER

The idea of a striving for power was very close to the conception of the masculine protest. Here masculine strength is equated with power and weakness with powerlessness. Whatever name one wished to give to this basic striving, it is deeply seated in human nature and the basic meaning was the will to dominate others. He found the direction toward power was particularly notable in the neurotics. Thus, at this stage of his thinking, the fictional final goal became identified with power. Likewise, it could take the form of a compensation for earlier feelings of inferiority. Here, Adler admits getting the idea of a will to power from Nietzche. One needs to remember, however, that as a psychiatrist, at this time, Adler was dealing mostly with neurotics, and, like Freud, he generalized his observations of the neurotics to normal individuals.

STRIVINGS FOR SUPERIORITY

Eventually, the dynamic force took on a new meaning which Adler identified as the striving for superiority or perfection. The nature of the dynamic force always meant a striving from "below" to "above." So the masculine protest or the striving for power were replaced by the striving for superiority. Later, the striving for superiority included the notions of self esteem and perfection.

Adler considered the basic notion of this dynamic force to be inborn. In a sense, it was the force of life itself. Although innate, its course had to be developed. Every person will actualize the basic motivational force in a different way. It is intimately related to the final goal and becomes the energizing force by which each person is going to reach that goal. The goal becomes a directing mechanism for the striving. The striving also can be interpreted as a striving for personal success. In the healthy individual, this personal striving becomes incorporated in part, taking on the form of *social interest*, or a concern beyond oneself in the form of a communal feeling or a striving for the betterment of others, indeed, for all of mankind (explained more in the following paragraphs).

The direction that the superiority striving will take is going to be influenced by the goal towards which it is intended. The striving also is intimately related to the feelings of inferiority. However, one thing should be made clear and is often the source of confusion in Adlerian psychology. Namely, the *strivings for superiority come first*, since this is inborn. The striving stems indirectly from the inferiority feelings. Here we have a situation in which we are *pushed* by our strivings *to overcome* our inferiority feelings, but, also *pulled*, by the strivings to be superior. Because both are involved in all people, it is difficult to keep them apart.

Everybody can not be superior in all ways, so each of us must find our particular way or ways in which we can be successful. Talent is not spread equally throughout the human race. Some people are over-endowed with many great potentialities. Others have few. Nevertheless, each of us must find some way in which we can be superior or at least a little better than someone else regardless of how insignificant that might be. One student might be a particularly skilled basketball player. Another might excel in some academic effort, still another might be a good musician. Other ways in which we might express our superiority could be in our particular choice of occupation; we could be a successful engineer, architect, professional athlete, scientist, lawyer, doctor, teacher, or minister. In business, we might be a good manager, salesman, accountant, or secretary. In trades, our superiority might take the form of a fine tailor, milliner, automobile mechanic, carpenter, plumber, or electrician. In the late middle ages, the guilds were formed including the master cobbler, baker, tailor, weaver, and blacksmith who had apprentices. Eventually, these became master craftsmen. Many other ways in life are often found for expressions of superiority, in cooking, gardening, housekeeping, nursing, rearing of children, or looking after the less fortunate.

Adler also pointed out that the direction the superiority striving takes may be the outcome of a particular organ inferiority. A visually handicapped person becomes an excellent scholar. A deaf person becomes a master craftsman. The strivings may be fulfilled through a variety of compensations. Several examples are given on pages 16-17. An element of perfection is in the basic strivings so in doing a particular task we do it in the best way we are able. It may not be absolutely perfect, but it could be a very good effort.

Of course, everybody does not succeed. The world is full of failures: neurotics, delinquents, alcoholics, suicides, sexually abnormal, and drug addicts. These people need help and the job of the therapist, the social worker, and the counselor is to redirect persons in such ways that their strivings for superiority can be achieved in a socially acceptable way. Other semi-failures may attempt to fulfill their strivings through exploiting and dominating others, in criminal acts, such as stealing and cheating or in punishing the inferior or weak. Consider the cases of child abuse or sexual molestation. Here the strivings have taken a pathological direction.

Adler also interpreted the strivings going from minus (-) to plus (+). As he put it: "The impetus from minus to plus never ends. The history of the human race points in the same direction . . . This not only states a fundamental category of thought, or a thought construct, but what is more, it represents the fundamental fact of our life" (Adler, 1956, p. 103).

SOCIAL INTEREST

In considering man as a unified whole, Adler also conceived that a person is related to a set of larger wholes: the family, the tribe, the community, or all of civilization. Man lacks the speed and power of most other animals. He does not have the strength of the carnivores or the sight and hearing necessary in the battle for survival in many species. Therefore, a human being can only maintain existence by maintaining a social life. In his book, *Understanding Human Nature*, Adler wrote:

> Social life became a necessity because through the community and the division of labor in which every individual subordinates himself to the group, the species was enabled to continue its existence. Division of labor (which means essentially civilization) alone is capable of making available to mankind those instruments of defense and offense which are responsible for all its possessions. (1927, p. 36)

Likewise, from the standpoint of nature, man is an inferior organism. The feeling of inferiority becomes an impetus for finding a way of adapting to nature.

Man does have a particular advantage over other animals in his capacity to develop a language. Speech becomes a product of communal living and creates a bond between the individual and others in the community. Here also one must consider the growing child's acquisition of language which he or she learns from those about him or her. Language is what enables a person to become a human personality.

Finally, in arguing for a need for a social world, Adler referred to the "rules of the game." These include education, superstition, totem and taboo, and laws. In early times, these were necessary to preserve the human race. Justice, as the brighter side of social living, is nothing more than the demands placed on members of a community in order to maintain the continued existence of the group.

THE DEVELOPMENT OF SOCIAL INTEREST

The term, *Geimenschaftsgefuhl*, in German presents some difficulty in translation into English. It has been translated in the following ways: social feeling, community feeling, communal intention, community interest, and *social interest*. This last translating, social interest, is the one most commonly used.

Freud had conceived man as basically selfish and narcissistic, that is, self-oriented. The pleasure principle was the basic principle of Freud's unconscious id, which involved the seeking of the individual's pleasure through the reduction of tension or pain caused by the unsatisfied instincts. The pleasure was an individual matter.

A contemporary of Freud, William McDougall, both in England and America also set forth an instinct doctrine. However, McDougall was a social psychologist and set forth his social psychology through his instinct theory. He never postulated a single social drive, but social behavior was accounted for by other instincts or a combination of them, such as maternal, paternal, gregariousness, constructiveness, acquiescence, and so on.

For Adler, however, social interest was a separate thing. Social interest was an innate aptitude to be responsive to the social situation. Incidentally, through his doctrine of social interest, Adler became the first of the *social analysts* to be followed by Karen Horney, Erich Fromm, and Harry Stack Sullivan. For these theorists the community, culture, and society took on greater importance than for Freud or Jung.

Social interest, as Adler conceived it, should not be considered as a *second dynamic force* along side the striving for superiority. It is part of a person's basic human nature and the striving for superiority sometimes can become incorporated into it, in that social interest needs a means of force to be expressed and accomplished.

Although social interest is inborn, it is only a potentiality and must be developed within a social context. It is not like breathing, which can occur entirely on its own. The first possibility for its development is with the mother. She nurses and cares for her offspring. She constitutes the beginning of a child's first social relationships. The father is the second most important, followed by the rest of the family constellation. Later on, the school and wider community become involved.

Part of the innate potentiality of social interest is being "other directed." This means a concern for and an interest in others. This does not mean one is merely social or sociable in a superficial way, as one who loves parties is a good mixer or an extrovert. It means much more; a feeling for the community and for social living. In the broadest sense, it involves a genuine concern for all mankind, a desire to be a socially useful person. It involves interest in others and the community and especially a concern for the improvement of the community and those who live in it.

Social interest may be beyond people. It may include other things such as animals and plants or even inanimate objects. It can involve an entire concern for the universe. This includes the concept of the ideal community which might be developed some time in the future.

Social interest becomes the main criterion for positive social adjustment. Adler stated: "Social interest is the barometer of the child's normality. The criterion which needs to be watched . . . is the degree of social interest which the child or individual maintains" (1956, p. 154).

Social interest is an extension of the self into the community. What one does is not mainly for himself or herself but for the community in which one is only a single member. The welfare of the community is the responsibility of every person who is a member of it. Individuals make a society and it is their responsibility to make it as perfect as possible. Social interest, then, includes a collective striving for superiority. So far the perfect community does not exist, so, at this point, approximations are as far as we can go. Society is constantly changing, so it is an individual matter to maintain an attitude of constant readaptation. Improvements in society are only brought about by those individuals who are the most adaptable and, in that sense, the most creative.

Social Interest and Intelligence

The degree of social interest is a function of how well a person can relate himself or herself to a given situation. Thus, social interest is an important part of a person's intellectual functioning. It is going to be related to an individual's solution to a problem. It thus becomes a part of what Adler called the "non-intellectual" factor of intelligence. What Adler meant by this is reason that is going to be useful or what we call "common sense."

In the following section, it will become clear that some people never develop social interest. These are the maladjusted, the people who have psychological problems. For a variety of reasons, their innate aptitude for social interest has been blocked or stunted. Adler considered the main reason for this to be a lack of proper preparation for life which should begin very early in infancy.

THOSE WHO LACK SOCIAL INTEREST

All failures—neurotics, psychotics, criminals, drunkards, problem children, suicides, perverts and prostitutes are failures because they are lacking in social interest. They approach the problems of occupation, friendship, and sex without the confidence that they can be solved by cooperation (Adler, 1956, p. 156).

The approach to life of these misfits is a private one. No one benefits by the consequences of their strivings, and their interests do not go beyond themselves. Their goals are always for a personal success or superiority, and if they have any successes, their accomplishments are limited to themselves. The meanings of their lives do not go beyond themselves, that is, their lives have no communicative values to others and they see no significance in their contributions to the lives of others.

Social interest is an absolute necessity for a successful solutions to the problems of life. One common factor in all maladjusted people is that they have little or no interest in others.

All failures in life begin as problem children. In Chapter 6, we shall discuss three faulty styles of life which inevitably begin in childhood. Adler identifies these as the inferior, the pampered and the neglected.

Criminals

Freud, Jung, and many of the later analysts paid little or no attention to the problems of crime and delinquency. On the other hand, Adler dealt with these problems in detail in many of his writings and personal practice. Problems of crime might arise out of improper compensations for organ inferiority, but this is not the most important factor, because too many people overcome or compensate for these inferiorities and become socially useful people. More likely they were never prepared for the development of a useful occupation. Usually, they never developed an ability to cooperate, a factor necessary for social interest. Poverty also might contribute to their problems. In many cases, they had no interest in work. Thus, they satisfy their strivings for superiority through criminal acts such as holding up a bank, carrying a concealed pistol, or through theft, burglary, or robbery. In reality, Adler considered them to be cowards who were unable to face the problems of life in a realistic way. Lacking social interest, the criminal cares little for others. He disregards the "rules of the game" because he has never learned them, that is, how to work and cooperate with others in a socially useful manner. The typical criminal has developed a superiority complex (see Ch. 2) for underlying massive feelings of inferiority. As a child, the criminal probably was the "getting type" (see next chapter). He may have been pampered or neglected.

Neurotics

In one of his earliest books, *The Neurotic Constitution* (1921), Adler developed his theory of neuroses. We shall deal in more detail in a later chapter on his theory of neurotic development. Here we will mention only a few relevant points. Besides lacking social interest, neurotics typically show a low level of activity (see next chapter). Like other conditions of maladjustment, neurotics suffer from either an inferiority or superiority complex. They have developed unsatisfactory safe guarding devices as protections against threats to their own self esteem. They may make up excuses, depreciate others or simply vacillate, being unable to make any decisions.

Prostitutes

In *The Practice and Theory of Individual Psychology* (1925), Adler outlined his interpretations of the behavior of prostitutes. He considered them to be the most explicit example of the rejections of the woman's role. He observed that prostitution is only possible in a society that has as one of its goals the satisfaction of men's needs and one which regards women as a basic means for satisfying the sexual desire. Yet, most men who visit prostitutes have a general contempt for them. In order to understand the psychology of prostitution, it is necessary to study (1) the men who go to prostitutes, (2) the pimps who secure their services, and (3) the prostitutes themselves. He regarded prostitutes as women who engage in "cheap tricks" which involve a means of least effort or resistance in order to elevate their own personalities through some act of sex. Prostitutes always have inferiority complexes. They lack a confidence in themselves (like criminals) which prevents them from entering a legitimate occupation. From childhood, they may have considered themselves worthless. Usually they had a tyrannical father and an oppressive mother. They are afraid of the true role of a woman. Prostitution becomes the only way in which they can face the problems of life. Prostitution is a means of gaining recognition, a means of gaining easy money and acquiring some feeling of superiority. Far from feeling womanly, the prostitute is primarily a frigid person. Through her attraction and sex, she gains superiority by degrading the man who pays her. For her and her partners, their fiction is a personal superiority. She degrades society rather than uplifting it.

Homosexuality and Other Sexual Deviations

Adler observed that *homosexuals* were typically dependent and pampered as children. In childhood, they were never prepared for the proper sexual role they were to play in adulthood. All homosexuals lack social interest and have inferiority complexes. The inferiority arises out of the uncertainty of their own sexual role. Adler denied that homosexuality had any basis in hereditary factors. Rather he linked homosexuality with a domineering attitude as a compensation for feelings of insecurity. Like other maladjusted people, homosexuals have never been able to solve the problems of *love*. Fearing defeat from the opposite sex, they solve their problems by excluding the opposite sex. A young boy fears a domineering mother. This fear generalizes to a rejection of all women. In girls, the same fear of a domineering mother gives rise to a rejection of her own sexual role of a woman.

In some instances, when a newborn arrives, the parents are disappointed in the sex of their child. Thus, they treat the newborn as if he or she were a member of the opposite sex by dressing the boy like a girl or vice versa. Adler pointed out that this attitude does not inevitably lead to homosexuality, but is a sign in the wrong direction.

Adler summed it up by saying that the homosexual is a discouraged person who had trained himself or herself to avoid defeat or any possibility that might lead to it by attempting to solve the love problem through the rejection of the opposite sex.

Like homosexuals, *sadists* and *masochists* are discouraged people with inferiority complexes. As children, they may have experienced excitement from hearing or reading of the brutalities in fairy tales. Later on, these fantasies can grow into realities. Masochists can produce their fear-excitement by ordering others, particularly, prostitutes to mistreat them. Sadists produce their fear-tension by identifying with their victims. In failing to solve their love problems, sadists feel superior in their cruelty to others. The masochists achieve their superiority by dictating to others how they may be hurt. They feel superior in spite of their submission to pain.

Adler concluded that all sexual perversions (his term) show themselves as compensatory strivings which operate as attempts to make up for feelings of inferiority. They over estimate the power of the opposite sex. Perversions are found in individuals who are oversensitive, ambitious, and defiant. The desire to be a "fellow player" is weak or absent with either a complete lack or great restriction of social interest (Adler, 1927).

Alder concluded that next to social interest, activity is the second most important personality trait (Ansbacher, 1977).

Combining social interest, or lack of it, and activity, or its lack, gives us a two dimensional personality theory and a fourfold typology of mankind. This will be discussed in the following chapter.

IMPLICATIONS

As we direct our behavior toward future goals, either real or fictional, some driving force is needed so as to give the push. The name of the striving is not so important as the recognition that it exists. In his writings, Adler gave it different names and finally settled on "strivings for superiority or self-enhancement." A worthwhile activity for each of us is to examine ways in which we fulfill these strivings. In our society we encourage achievement. What are the ways in which people achieve some degree of superiority? Those ways may involve financial success, being a good student, getting ahead in our vocation, being a good athlete, a superior card player, a social success, a scholar, an artist, lawyer, doctor, politician, or craftsman. Our strivings can be fulfilled in our job, our dealings with other people and our relationships with the opposite sex. Adler's psychology considered each person as unique, so each of us will fulfill our strivings in many different ways. Feelings of inferiority can also help us give the push to overcome. The song, "We Shall Overcome" is an expression of these strivings among minority groups. Adler was very much concerned with the equality of the sexes. The "equal rights" movement is a manifest expression of the strivings by groups of individuals who have been discriminated against. In women he later called it the "masculine protest."

Arising out of these strivings is a concern which Adler called "social interest." This is an inborn potential but has to be nurtured. Everyone does not necessarily express social interest. Maladjusted people, criminals, drug addicts, alcoholics, prostitutes, sexual deviants all lack social interest. The selfish ones, the egotists, the self-centered people who are only concerned for themselves lack social interest. Adler considered social interest to be one of his most important concepts.

Typically, well adjusted people have a concern for children, the family, friends as well as the needy, the homeless, and the down trodden. In our gifts to charitable organizations and other worthwhile causes we are expressing our social interest, a concern for the help and betterment of many organizations and people in our society.

A friend said to me recently, "I never realized until well into my middle life what my final goal was even though it was set much earlier; that is, to make some lasting contribution to society. I may never achieve it, but it's a nice thought to have."

DEGREES OF ACTIVITY AND PERSONALITY TYPES

Unlike Jung, Adler did not consider himself primarily as a type theorist because in his Individual Psychology, he considered every person to be a unique human being, so no two people are alike. Yet, when he introduced the concept *degrees of activity* and combined it with social interest or lack of it, certain personalities tended to fall into different groups of categories, leading to a kind of typology, which is one of the considerations of this chapter. A leading authority on Adlerian psychology, (Ansbacher & Ansbacher, 1956) noted, that apparently Adler did not consider degrees of activity as one of his most important concepts. Adler did not write as extensively on this subject as he did on social interest, strivings for superiority, compensation, feelings of inferiority, and so forth.

On the other hand, Ansbacher (1977, p. 61) wrote, "Activity is after social interest the second most important personality trait." If we take these two personality characteristics, we come up with a two dimensional theory. Furthermore, if we distinguish people who have either high or a low degree of activity along with those with a high or low social interest, we find a system with four different personality types.

In the previous chapter, we discussed strivings for superiority and social interest which are not synonymous concepts but may be related. To these two, we add degrees of activity, we end up with a third personality trait.

Adler got his idea of degrees of activity from physics in which movement occurs in both time and space. Movement involves energy which operates in both space and time. Applying this to psychology, the space refers to the social organization or many social groups in which human beings find themselves. Human activity also involves time in which one's actions may be fast or slow.

Although Adler did not attempt to describe degrees of activity in any quantitative way as might be done by an experimental psychologist who measures the rate of a particular response, the following example frequently referred to a certain objectivity with regard to action. A child who runs away from home or a boy who starts a fight in the street expresses a higher degree of activity than the child who sits at home and reads a book. Adler further noted that the degree of activity is acquired in childhood and remains relatively constant throughout life. Active children will become active adults. Here we have activity as movement whether one expresses a lot of it, or a minimal amount as in a phlegmatic person (see discussion under "Four Temperaments" later in this chapter).

Yet, there is a certain subjectivity to Adler's psychology. Thus, degrees of activity also may be regarded in a more subjective way. Here Adler makes reference to a person's attitudes toward himself or herself as well as the world about him or her. A positive opinion of oneself and the world about would imply a higher degree of activity than would a negative one. Neurotics and psychotics, for example, express a low degree of activity and quite obviously they have a low opinion of themselves and the world about them. Adler places these people typically in his group called the "avoiding type."

While a high degree of social interest is always considered a positive factor, high activity can be either positive or negative. Those with high social interest are always social and useful individuals, but those with a high degree of activity may or may not have high social interest. For example, one may consider children who are characteristically stubborn and quarrelsome as having a high degree of activity as compared to the shy, reticent or dependent child. The actively troublesome child can be just as great a problem as the one who is continually fearful.

People who commit crimes or suicides were, as children, highly active (Adler, 1956). On the other hand, sexual perverts may have had either a high or low degree of activity as children. But socially useful and courageous people always have a high degree of activity.

All of human existence is going to involve some degree of activity, whether it be high or low. Likewise, the degree of activity gives us some indication of a person's style or life (see Chapter 6). From observing the movements of a child Adler felt he could predict the degree of activity with which that person would someday face the later problems of life (Adler, 1938). Despite the endless variations in individuals' behavior, a general and uniform degree of activity assessed.

TYPOLOGY

By taking into account the variables of low activity and high and low social interest, we can come up with a theory of four different types of personality. In an article in the International Journal of Individual Psychology in 1933, Adler set out his typology based on the combination of activity and social interest as shown in Figure 5.1.

	High Social Interest	**Low Social Interest**
High Activity	Socially useful person	Ruling person
Low Activity	————————	Getting person Avoiding person

Figure 5.1. Adler's typology of personality based on the combination of activity and social interest (Lundin, 1985).

The Ruling Person

Adler described the ruling person as high activity with low social interest as follows, "Thus we find individuals whose approach to reality show from early childhood through their entire lives, a more or less dominant ruling attitude. This attitude appears in all their relationships" (Adler, 1929a, p. 68). He went on to describe the ruling type to include individuals who are alcoholics, drug addicts, delinquents, tyrants, and sadists. Here reference is made to Shakespeare's, Richard III, who says, "And therefore, since I can not be a lover, I am determined to prove a villain." These people may make attacks on others or on themselves for the purpose of hurting others. The more active they are, the more direct will be their attacks. They achieve their superiority by hurting and exploiting.

The Getting Type

This type shows both low activity and low social interest. Adler considered this to be the most frequent type. These people expect everything from others and give nothing in return. Like the ruling type, they are unable to solve life's problems in any satisfactory way. Ordinarily, their relationships with others is passive. If they have any charm, they will use it to persuade others to help them, and like the ruling type, they lack any ability to cooperate.

The Avoiding Type

This type also lacks social interest and has a low level of activity. Instead of struggling with the problems of life, the avoiding type attempts to sidestep them. Their lack of self confidence creates a chasm between them and other people. In this group, Adler typically placed the neurotics and psychotics. The latter may include those people who may have completely withdrawn themselves from the world of reality.

The Socially Useful Type

This fourth type has both a high activity level and high social interest. Their activity is seen in the benefit of others. They are prepared to cooperate and use their abilities for the benefit of mankind. They are conscious of the needs of others and contribute to the benefit of the community. Of the four types, this is the only one where the people are psychologically healthy. Concerning this type, Adler wrote, "It is useful, normal, highly embedded in the stream of evolution of mankind" (1956, p. 168).

High Social Interest
and Low Activity

Note that no type is in the quadrant of high social interest and low activity. Adler's conception here is that no such personality can exist. High social interest must involve some degree of activity. Without activity, social interest can not function or be expressed. On the other hand, it is possible, as Adler has pointed out, that one can have a high degree of activity without social interest, as in the case of the ruling personality.

THE FOUR TEMPERAMENTS

Some years before Adler developed his type theory of personality, he had attempted to relate the four temperaments of Hippocrates and Galen to his own personality theory.

Hippocrates, in about 400 B.C., had established the idea of the four humors in the body and had related them to the four elements of the universe as set down by Empedocles about fifty years earlier. Empedocles had stated that the four elements of the universe were earth, air, fire, and water. Hippocrates then related these to the four humors of the body: blood, phlegm, black bile, and yellow bile. From these, the Roman physician Galen took the next steps to relate the four humors to the four basic human conditions as follows:

blood: sanguine (cheerful) personality

phlegm: phlegmatic personality

yellow bile: choleric (fiery) personality

black bile: melancholic personality

Adler, in a way, related these four to his own personality typology as follows:

Sanguine (cheerful personality) .... socially useful type

Choleric (fiery personality) .... ruling type

Melancholic .... avoiding type

Phlegmatic .... getting type

The *sanguine personality* shows a joy in living, an appreciation of the pleasant part of life; one who appreciates happy events and has less inferiority feelings. The sanguine has a positive attitude towards life. He or she becomes the socially useful person.

The *choleric personality* has a wildness of disposition. As related to Individual Psychology, the person with choleric personality is the one with strong strivings for power, is highly active and aggressive. He or she becomes the ruling personality.

The *melancholic person* is sad, reflective, and backward looking. He or she lacks confidence to overcome difficulties, thinks more of self than of others, disregards the positive possibilities of life, and moves backwards rather than forward. This is closely related to the avoiding type.

The *phlegmatic personality* lacks energy and activity, seems indifferent to life, lacks interest, and makes no effort to get involved in life's situations, is slow and sluggish, and receives rather than gives. This person corresponds most closely to the getting personality.

SUMMARY

Since Adler considered degrees of activity as an important personality characteristic, a discussion of activity seems logically to follow that of social interest. Adler established a kind of personality typology. Remember that this was merely a convenient way of characterizing some people and presented an understanding of how social interest, or its lack, and activity could be related.

Activity and social interest as well as many of the concepts heretofore mentioned all contribute to what Adler called the "style of life," which is the general pattern of living. The style of life is, for each of us, unique. In the following chapter, we shall consider the development of life style along with certain styles which Adler considered faulty.

IMPLICATIONS

Next to strivings for superiority and social interest, Adler considered degrees of activity to be of special importance. A child with much physical energy is described as having a high degree of activity while one who sits alone looking at a comic book would be characterized as having low activity. Of course, degrees of activity need not be limited to the physical. People with lots of new ideas and inspirations can be considered as having high activity.

Adler also distinguished between high and low social interest. Being involved with and assisting other people rank high in social interest while the self centered person manifests low social interest.

The socially useful person exhibits both high activity and high social interest. A person with low activity can not express high social interest. Typically, tyrants, despots, bossy, author- itarian people can have high activity but low social interest. Finally, two kinds of people manifest both low activity and low social interest. These are the demanding or getting personalities who want much and give little along with the recluse or avoiding personalities.

We should all aim to be socially useful people expressing care and concern for others and doing something about it.

and explicitly expressed. It can most easily be discovered or altered in life by a reference to earliest memories (see the following). Whether these memories are true or not does not matter; they still will give a clue to the style of life. The life style of the child or the adult is interpreted in accordance with one's own view of the world. It is expressed in practically every aspect of our behavior; in thinking, emotions, and actions. The direction of the life style is selected by the individual and his or her internal strivings.

As the style of life is set in early childhood, in a general way, it usually remains unchanged. This is not to say that change is impossible, for people who have developed faulty styles of life are in need of change, which, in many cases, may be the job of the therapist or counselor.

As an example of the early formation of the style of life, Adler makes reference to the setting of his own style of life in the following statement:

> When I was five, I became ill with pneumonia and was given up by the physician. A second physician advised a treatment just the same, and in two days I became well again . . . From that time on, I recall always thinking of myself in the future as a physician. This means that I had set a goal from which I could expect an end to my childlike distress, fear of death. Clearly I expected more from the occupation of my choice than it could accomplish. The overcoming of death and the fear of death is something I should not have expected from human, but only from divine accomplishment. Reality, however, demands action and so I was forced to modify my goal by changing conscious forms of my guiding future until it appeared to satisfy reality. (Adler, 1931, pp. 29-30)

In Adler's strongly teleological approach, the style of life is determined by the individual's creative power. Each person is endowed with a freedom to create his or her own style of life. Each of us is responsible for what we are and how we behave. This power puts us in control of our own lives. It also sets the final goal and contributes to the ways we are going to achieve that goal.

However, Adler did not completely ignore heredity and environment but placed much less importance to them than did

Freud, Horney, and other analysts. Heredity is responsible for our unique physical make up. Environment will operate in many respects whereby we are going to achieve that goal. Likewise, order of birth cannot be ignored. We are all much more than the product of our heredity and environment. In our creative self we are able to act on the environment and make it react on us. We use our heredity and environment as a means by which we construct our own personality. Heredity and environment are analogous to the raw materials out of which we construct a house, but the architecture of the house is of our own making. So each of us must decide how the structure is to be made. The building can be beautifully constructed or end up as an ugly and impractical place in which to dwell.

The creative power (self) gives us complete freedom (as opposed to determinism). We have a freedom of will to choose. Psychologically healthy people make good decisions. Their final goals are a matter of their own choosing.

In his book, *The Science of Living* (1929a), Adler used the analogy of the "low doorway" to illustrate how the creative power of the maladjusted (neurotic) can be compared with the normal person. Suppose you were to walk through a doorway that was four feet high. You might bend down far enough to pass through the doorway successfully. This would be the technique that the healthy person would use. On the other hand, you might bump your head, fall back, and bump it again. This would be the approach of the maladjusted. Both people had the creative power to stoop down or bump their heads. The healthy person will choose the correct solution, the neurotic, the wrong one.

DISCOVERING THE STYLE OF LIFE

As Adler described in his account of how he decided to become a physician (p. 59), what can be deducted is that early childhood experiences with which one is to cope along with the attitudes we develop toward them are of utmost importance in shaping the style of life. These are to be found in attitudes and moods toward others; illnesses; relations with our families; particularly our mother and father; and friends. Later on, we may observe the style of life being expressed in our occupation, the ways in which we deal with our associates, with society, and with our love affairs. The life style we set is reflected in our habits of eating and sleeping, and in the ways a person behaves. One not only observes a person's actions in ordinary situations, but in critical circumstances as well. Clues to the style of life may be found in more subjective areas as in one's dreams (see Ch. 8) and early memories. These more subjective events are less under the control of reality.

EARLY MEMORIES

Adler felt strongly that early memories could give explicit clues to discovering an individual's life style. He routinely asked his patients to report the first things they could remember in childhood.

This apparent random discovery of the past seemed deeply significant, just as a dream would be. The first memory also may be supplemented by early memories of parents and siblings. The more specific memories suggest attitudes concerning the life style. The earliest memories are significant because they represent a subjective starting point revealing the rudiments of the life style. Sometimes the memories will be correct recollections, but at other times they may be mere fantasy. Whether they are real images or false, Adler felt they revealed important meanings which could give clues to the real life style.

In this context Adler wrote:

> The active work of his memory guided by his style of life selects an event which gives a strong indication of his individual tendency. The pampered child is revealed by the fact that the memory recalls a situation that included the solicitous mother. But a still more important fact is discovered. *He looked on while other people worked.* His preparation for life is that of an onlooker. (Adler, 1938, p. 213)

Early memories reveal the individual's fundamental view of life. They are the first real formation of fundamental attitudes. They give us an opportunity to see at one glance what one has taken as a starting point of our development. Adler maintained that most people consider the first memories as mere facts and do not realize the meaning that is hidden in them.

Examples of how Adler was able to discover the style of life through early recollections appear in a number of his writings. Here are three examples from *What Life Should Mean to You* (1931).

1. A woman recalled her earliest memory of attending her grandfather's funeral when she was three years old. She remembered viewing him in the coffin. She also recalled the grave and seeing the coffin lowered into the ground.

    Adler's interpretation was that the woman was very impressed with the fact of death, also that her grandfather was very fond of her and probably spoiled her as grandparents frequently do. Adler concluded: "What we have learned from her memory as a whole is that her grandfather was friendly to her and that she is a visual type, and that death plays a great role in her mind. The meaning she has drawn from life is 'We all must die'" (Adler, 1931. p. 79).

2. Another woman recalled that when she was four years old her great-grandmother came to visit. During the visit, the family had a four generation picture taken. Her brother and she also had their pictures taken. Her brother was placed on the arm of a chair and given a ball to hold while she stood on the other side of the chair, but was given nothing. "We were both asked to smile," she recalled. "My brother did, but I couldn't."

    From this description Adler concluded the following: (a) The woman is very much interested in her pedigree. (b) She is very much bound up in her family. (c) She feels a strong family preference for her brother. (d) She is probably not well adjusted. Adler suggested that if a person's earliest recollections are unpleasant, the style of life is going to be of a negative sort. If the earliest recollections are happy ones, the style of life also will be pleasant and optimistic.

What also should be pointed out is that those early memories do not determine the life style but are merely expressions of it which have already been shaped by one's creative self.

3. Perhaps the most often referred to example from the same book is that of a woman who recalled receiving a pony as a gift from her father when she was three years old. Her sister also received a pony as a gift. Her sister took the straps of the animal from her father and rode the pony in great triumph down the pathway. Her own pony followed, but it ran too fast for her to handle and she was thrown into the dirt below. She also mentioned that eventually she became a better horsewoman than her sister, but never forgot the humiliation of being surpassed by her sister and her own downfall.

Adler's interpretation is that she was not particularly happy in her home life, because her first recollection was of her father, rather than her mother, which would ordinarily have been the case for most people. Furthermore, her mother probably favored her sister. The initial triumph of her older sister implied an unhealthy competition between the two girls, a relationship in which she believed she was more humiliated and discriminated against. The fact that she later recalled that she eventually surpassed her sister as a horsewoman did not diminish her initial feelings about her sister. Thus, the strivings of the second child to overcome the first child is a constant theme in Adler's writings. (See the next section, "Order of Birth.")

Adler used early recollections as one of his therapeutic techniques since one of the aims of the therapist is to alter an undesirable style of life. The question often arises, do early recollections change as therapy progresses and the style of life is altered by therapeutic procedures? The general answer seems to be yes.

ORDER OF BIRTH

Adler placed considerable emphasis on the order of birth in the family constellation as a contributing factor to the style of life and to the whole matter of personality development. By birth order he meant one's chronological position in the family constellation. Basically, he identified four main possibilities: (1) the first born, (2) the second born (often called the middle child), (3) the last born, and (4) the only child.

The First Born

The first child occupies a very unique position. He or she starts out as an only child, one on whom the parents ordinarily will shower all their love and attention. He or she is a pioneer, the first one to travel the birth canal, the first on whom the parents will have to learn how to bring up a child. In the beginning, the first child is the center of attention. Then, a shocking event occurs. Another child, a brother or sister, comes into the world and into the family constellation. Unless the parents have been careful to prepare this older child for the newcomer into the family by still giving sufficient attention, problems may develop. As the second child enters the family, the first born, as Adler puts it, becomes the "dethroned king." This dethronement will intensify the ordinary normal feelings of inferiority. This kind of unpreparedness for the arrival of a second child may lead the older child later in life to become a neurotic, alcoholic, criminal, or sexual deviant. It probably will lead to strivings for power in a variety of ways including aggression and vanity in a struggle to regain the lost empire.

On the more positive side, the first born is more likely to become a leader since the younger siblings are weaker. The first born will understand, better than the younger, the significance of authority, because earlier in life they had power, then lost it, and must strive to regain it. Having suffered the loss, the possibility exists that the first born may be more sympathetic towards the younger ones in the family.

The oldest child will tend to have a greater concern for the past which was reminiscent of the time when he or she was the unopposed "king" or "queen." In terms of Adler's typology, if the first born does not become a socially useful person, he or she is most likely to become the "ruling type."

The Second Born
or Middle Child

The most likely characteristic of the second born is competition. Their lives are a continuous race to catch up. They are runners in a race for life. Adler reported that they had common dreams of running. In some instances the attitude "if you can't beat them, join them" also might lead to an attitude of strong cooperation. On the other hand, the attitude of competition could be so strong that they become revolutionaries. Most likely, the competitive attitude will operate within reason. In general, Adler considered the second born to be in a favorable position and least likely to develop personality disorders. (One needs to recall that Adler, himself, was the second born.)

The Last Born

The youngest child is most likely to be the pampered one. In many cases, the parents realize that this will be their last child. The older ones are growing up so they can indulge and spoil the last child giving all they have, psychologically, to the last one. Because of the greater possibility of spoiling, Adler considered the last child to be the problem child. Likewise, because of the spoiling, the last child is more likely to be overly dependent.

On the most positive side, Adler cited cases where the last born strives to excel and to surpass the older ones to become the conquering hero. He cited many fairy tales where the youngest becomes the winner. However, because of the greater possibility of spoiling, Adler believed "the second largest proportion of problem children come from the youngest" (Adler, 1931, p. 151).

The Only Child

Like the youngest child, the only child is most likely to be pampered. Maybe because the mother is afraid of losing her only child, or for whatever reason, the parents may realize that they are able to have only one offspring. The only child is not likely to be the competitor, because there is no one to compete with in the family. As only children, they may become the center of attention and may develop exaggerated opinions of their own importance. Adler contended that only children are typically timid and dependent. His reasoning was that the parents are typically anxious, perhaps about having another child or fearing that they will lose the only one they have. This attitude is communicated to the offspring.

Some Research Findings

A number of psychologists have attempted to test the validity of some of Adler's assumptions regarding the order of birth. A survey of the literature by Herrill (1972) regarding the relationship between order of birth and the power structure in the armed forces was made. In his survey, he found among Army generals and Navy admirals that the percentage of first born far exceeded the probabilities to be found in the general population. In another study in his survey, 67% of superior Navy jet pilots and 80% of "achiever" pilots in the Air Force were first born. Herrell's third observation concerned the dethronement of the first born. Here he found several studies which indicated that the first born were "over represented in the military psychiatric hospitals."

A study by Mellilo (1983) found a striking positive correlation between birth order and intellectual performance in nearly 400,000 cases in the Netherlands, that is to say, the first born are likely to be more intelligent. In a series of studies reported by Rychman (1985), the first born were over represented among college students, graduate students, university faculty members, and people in science and government.

In a review of 27 studies, Barry and Blane (1977) reported birth order and alcoholism. In 20 of the studies, the highest percentage of alcoholics were the last born. Although this is contrary to Adler's original statement (see page 64), it does support the hypothesis that the last born are more likely to be pampered and dependent children, and in these cases, their dependence becomes one on alcohol. In conclusion, Rychman

(1985) wrote: "Nevertheless, the research findings have generally supportive of much of Adler's theorizing and res on birth order effects continues at an unprecendented rate (p. 103).

FAULTY STYLES OF LIFE

While Adler maintained that most people create their own maladjustments, sometimes factors within the person or in the environment also can participate in the difficulties. Therefore, he identified three faulty styles of life: (1) the inferior, (2) the pampered, and (3) the neglected.

The Inferior Style of Life

This ordinarily comes about because of exaggerated organ inferiorities. Whether these are genetic, or the result of disease or injury, the inferiority itself it not a single sufficient factor. The exaggerated inferiority complex will arise out of it. Everyone has some general inferiority feelings (see Ch. 2), but an organic inferiority simply adds to the burden. While many people compensate in extremely desirable ways, the possibility still exists that unfortunate compensations may lead to extreme maladjustment. The following are examples from this author's own experience.

1. A member of my fraternity when I was in college was extremely short in stature, being 5 feet 3 inches tall. This is very short in comparison to other men whose average height is 5 feet 8 or 9 inches tall. His compensation took the form of arrogance, defiance, hostility, and egocentricity. He gave the impression that he was the final authority on everything, whether it be science, art, or etiquette. As a senior in college, he treated the freshman pledges as if they were dirt under his feet. He bossed them, criticized them, and ordered them about as if they were his slaves. I remember one day as I was standing at a window along with another freshman friend seeing him come up the walk to the front door. My friend said to me, "Some day, I'll fix that arrogant bastard." I also recall that at the end of my

freshman year when room mates for the next year were chosen, this short junior asked me if I would care to room with him. He told me that my own personality needed to be improved and he was the one to do it. Fortunately, another friend and I had already decided to room together. I did tell him, however, that I was perfectly content with my personality the way it was.

2. Some others with organ inferiorities might express even more extreme undesirable behavior. I knew of a boy who had a leg injury which caused him to limp and could not keep up with the others while walking down the street. He was defiant and carried a switch blade which he used as a threat in any case of an aggressive confrontation. He was caught in a robbery of a drug store (presumably for illegal drugs) and was sentenced to prison. While behind bars, he killed another prisoner in an attack with a knife and was sentenced to death. This is a very common story, and the literature is filled with similar cases of delinquents and criminals who suffer from inferiority complexes related to organ inferiorities.

3. Sometimes people with organ inferiorities will attempt to hide their handicap. I knew of a man who was born with only one ear lobe. As he grew up, he wore his hair long enough so that it covered both his ears. Attempting to hide the inferior organ led to exaggerated feelings of inferiority less his secret be discovered. The result was a low self-esteem, a lack of social interest, and cowardice. Adler (1927) made reference to people who try to hide their handicap and feel they are living among enemies. They fear defeat more than they desire success.

4. The inferior life style can also take the form of a superiority complex (see Ch. 2). I had a one time friend who came from very poor economic circumstances. He also had a heart condition which exempted him from serving in the armed forces during World War II. Leading from his modest background, he was determined to cultivate the rich. Eventually, he met a rich widow, without children, who was twenty years his senior. He

escorted her to the opera, symphony concerts, and other cultural events which she enjoyed. He gave up his job as an undertaker's assistant and became her constant companion. They spent the winters in Palm Beach, Florida and the summers in Bar Harbor, Maine. She had very strong social connections, and he learned to imitate the ways of the socially prominent. He became ego-centric and vain. His clothes were expensive, but gaudy. They were purchased by his rich widow friend. He would wear a bright yellow jacket with purple trousers. He became a leech on his lonely companion. As she reached old age and needed help in getting around, he prayed every night that she might soon pass away. Since she had no living relatives, he finally persuaded her to make him the sole heir to her fortune. Adler would have placed him in the "getting" type. He not only lacked social interest, but was a completely socially useless person. Eventually she died, but, ironically, the next year he developed cancer and died six months later, so he was never able to enjoy the money he had waited so long to inherit.

The Pampered Style of Life

In his book, *Social Interest* (1938), Adler devoted a chapter entitled, "The Unreal World of the Pampered." Discussions of pampering or spoiling also appear in many of Adler's other writings (Adler 1921, 1927, 1931, 1938). The pampered style of life is undoubtedly the most common of the faulty styles because more children are apt to be spoiled or pampered than neglected. The pampered child lacks social interest and has a low activity level. Thus, these people will either be of the "getting" or "avoiding" type (see Figure 5.1). In many cases, the pampered style of life is the key to the neuroses (see Ch. 10). Pampered children expect others to look after them. They wish to be protected and catered to. Their selfish demands become their primary motivating force. As adults, they expect the world to spoil them, just as their mothers did when they were children. Pampering is expressed in the three problems of life (see Ch. 7), which are society, occupation, and love. Their attitude is of extreme egocentricity. They usually have few friends, if any, because their attitude is "what can you do for me rather than what I can do for you." In love and sex relations, the same holds true. Sexual intercourse is only for their own pleasure without any regard for the desires of their sex partner. Their aspirations in their job are completely personal without regard for the benefit of others with whom they work or their company.

The pampered child does not suffer from too much love, but from overprotection and indulgence. Consequently, they never learn self-reliance or self-confidence. Even as children, they may use pathological techniques such as temper tantrums, bed wetting, or acute anxiety to gain their insatiable desires for sympathy and attention.

The Oedipus Complex. Unlike Freud, Adler did not interpret the Oedipus complex as a universal aspect of development nor based on the sexual instinct. When it does occur, it is the result of pampering. Sometimes the pampering on the part of the mother may be the result of the mother's excessive coddling or the father's indifference. In other cases, it arises out of the mother's desire to induce the boy to side with her against the father.

As a result of overprotection and indulgence the child becomes tied to the mother. In other instances, the reverse is true and the pampering of the girl is the result of the father's preference.

In *Social Interest* (1938), Adler wrote, "Freud's so-called Oedipus complex, which seems to him to be the natural foundation of psychical development, is nothing more than *one of the many forces that appear in the life of the pampered child* who is the helpless sport of his excited fantasies" (p. 51).

The Neglected Style of Life

The neglected style of life is created by those children who feel unwanted and rejected. They feel the love typically rendered by their parents is lacking. In extreme cases, they feel hatred. Of course, if a child has received in infancy some degree of care and attention, he or she can not feel totally rejected because enough care was given on the part of someone to allow the person to survive. Characteristically, the neglected child probably was unwanted. Often children raised in institutions, such as orphanages where the care is minimal, are more likely to develop a neglected style of life. Perhaps the family is very large and some of the less fortunate will be neglected.

In some cases, neglected children have been abused either physically or psychologically. They may have been battered or belittled. Recently, much has been written about the abused child. What has been fairly well established is that adults who are child abusers were abused when they were children.

This style of life is expressed in a spitefulness towards others. Even in childhood, they are uncooperative and lacking normal positive feelings. Never having been given affection, their attitude as adults will be deficient in any love of others.

Like the other faulty styles of life, they will lack social interest. Their level of activity can either be high or low so they could end up being the ruling type or either the getting or avoiding type.

Along with hate, the neglected seek revenge. They view the world as their enemy. Consequently, in time, they become hostile towards their environment. Their arrogance makes them difficult people with whom to work. They may be the gripers, the complainers, and tend to generally sour about life.

In many instances, the characteristics of the neglected child are similar to the pampered. The basic difference is that they are more difficult to deal with.

Adler summed up the characteristics of the neglected child in the following way

> Such a child (the neglected) has never known what love and cooperation can be: he makes up an interpretation of life which does not include these friendly forces. It will be understood that when he faces the problems of life, he will overrate their difficulty and understate this own capacity to meet them with the aid and good will of others. He has found society to be cold to him and he will expect it always to be cold. Especially he will not see that he can win affection and esteem by actions which are useful to others. He will thus be suspicious of others and unable to trust himself. (1931, p. 170)

Adler also suggested that the neglected child would like to be pampered.

Whether the style of life is healthy or faulty, Adler felt that we all have to face certain problems in life: (1) our dealings with society which includes all the people around us, (2) our occupation, and (3) love and marriage. These three problems are the subject for the following chapter.

IMPLICATIONS

An understanding of the style of life includes many of Adler's basic concepts and may be expressed in many different ways. It includes the ways in which we attack life's problems, our goals and compensations, the means whereby we fulfill our superiority strivings and express social interest. Since all of these are individual matters, everyone has a unique style of life.

A helpful procedure is for each of us to discover our own style of life. Adler gives us some hints as to how we may be able to discover it. Our style is set by each of us at a very early age. Of course if the life style is faulty, we can alter it. One way of discovering the style of life is to observe an individual's behavior, in particular, how a person interacts with others.

Another way is to look into our earliest memories. A young man in his middle twenties who was plagued with chronic anxiety and phobias recalled an earliest memory of being very fearful of his mother's noisy vacuum cleaner. A woman who felt lonely and self conscious in the presence of others recalled an early childhood of loneliness with no other children with whom to play. She had to play by herself. A successful trial lawyer recalled a continuous battle with his father. A socialite's earliest memories were of going to many birthday parties. A vice president in charge of sales remembered his favorite pastime of playing "store." It does not matter whether or not the memories are real. What is important is that these were the memories. When Adler overhead the doctor say, "Your child is lost," he was determined that he would grow up to be a good doctor. This was a bad doctor.

Another way of finding our life style is through an analysis of our dreams. Recurrent dreams are of particular importance. Adler did not propose fixed or strict interpretations. Each individual is to figure out what the dream means. A man who suffered severe inferiority feelings because of poor eyesight had recurrent dreams of being lost on the streets of a large city or sometimes losing his wife or children. They would disappear from the dream and he would never find them before he awakened.

Adler identified three faulty styles of life: the inferior, the pampered, and the neglected. The inferior may result from inadequate compensations for organ defects or environmental mishaps. Criminals frequently have inferiority complexes. Pampering or spoiling inhibits the proper development of social interest. The spoiled child sees himself or herself as the center of the universe. A man who was overindulged as an only child took to heavy drinking in his teens, eventually went through three divorces, and engaged in "shady" deals in his business.

The neglected style of life can result from either physical or psychological neglect. Often the neglected grows up to become spiteful and hateful of others. For example, a man who at an early age was in a family that went through a messy divorce. His mother cared little for the children who were put in the care of indifferent nurse maids. He never knew what care and love were all about. At his job as a personnel director he was a troublemaker. He delighted in causing inconvenience for those about him. He gossiped, talked behind peoples' backs, and went out of his way to cause unnecessary trouble for those other employees who had no connection with his office. As one would deduct, he had to change jobs frequently.

In counseling, part of the job of the therapist is to discover the faulty style of life and help the individual patient to correct the faulty style of life by replacing it with a more effective one.

THREE PROBLEMS
OF LIFE

OUR RELATIONS WITH SOCIETY,
OUR OCCUPATION, AND
LOVE AND MARRIAGE

Adler suggested that certain ties bind individuals together and these ties are best expressed in the three problems of life. None of these can be solved separately; but each requires an interrelationship with the other two: the three problems involve a person's relationship to society, which, of course, involves social interest, one's job or occupation, and the relationships in love and marriage. The successful solutions to all of these problems are going to involve social interest.

SOCIETY

The first tie that binds mankind together is that we all belong to the human race. We live together with others of our own kind and most of us live in association with other people. The first problem involves a concern for society, in particular, our own community which includes a concern for others, friendships and cooperation. With the solution to this problem, we are then prepared to handle the other two, our occupation and our love relationships. Life would be extremely difficult if every person attempted to make a living all by himself or herself with no cooperation or reliance on the efforts of the past which have led to the creation of a civilization as we know it today. No healthy person can become detached from the community. We are all at the mercy of the natural world with all its advantages, allowing us to grow our crops, satisfy our needs for survival in providing food and drink as well as the disadvantages in pestilence, storms and floods, earthquakes, famine, and sudden climatic changes. Consequently, mankind, through the ages, has grouped together in families, clans, and tribes. Together these groups fought the dangers of the natural world.

Cooperation became the key to survival. Laws were created to control our activities and punish those who acted in defiance of the common good of the community. Each person's life became a matter of adjustment to the group. Language developed to aid humankind in the adjustment to the community.

The matter of mutual concern begins at birth with the relationship between the mother and child. Through the mutual cooperation in feeding and caring, the infant survives. As the child grows older, he or she is taught cooperation with others.

As civilization evolved, people became educated. Schools were established and the children learned an interest in others. Adler stressed the need to instill courage in children so they could master the frustrations which are the necessary outcomes of communal living. Through courage and cooperation, we become linked with our fellow human beings.

Adler stressed the fact that those who regard others as their enemies lack courage and will have a difficult time succeeding in the group. Over and over again he referred to pampering (see previous chapter) as one of the most dev-astating conditions leading to adult maladjustment. Pampering inhibits interest in others, so the pampered child has few friends. Pampering leads only to self interest and uncooperative behavior. Without cooperation, a group or social unit cannot survive. Often one can simply look or talk with a person to discover if he or she has a pampered style of life. Indications are unfriendly glances, an empty facial expression, or a failure to listen, particularly when unpleasant matters are discussed. What others think or do is of no interest to the pampered person. Ways of shaking hands or moving about reveal how well a pampered person is able to make contact with others.

Adler suggested a dichotomy into which all people can be placed (1) those who live for others and give of their own free time to the community and (2) those who live only for themselves. Of course, some individuals' social interest is limited only to their immediate family or those who contribute to the community but have no concern for single individuals. In this day of modern technology, people are brought closer together: by fast air travel, radio, TV, and direct-dialing telephones. These bring nations closer. International trades makes one group more dependent on another but allows for a greater cooperation between nations. The tremendous earthquake in Mexico City and the terrible famine in Ethiopia are illustrations. Adler would have been heartened to know how the people of other nations are contributing their efforts in giving food, money, and personal services for the survival of these unfortunate people.

With regard to a person's relationship to his or her society, Adler stressed the development of individuals' abilities for their own good and the good of the community rather than mere self sacrifice.

OCCUPATION

When people learned to cooperate, then came the possibility for the discovery of a division of labor. Through this division one group can work for the advantage of others. Some people attempt to solve the problem of occupation by doing no work at all; but, in avoiding the problem, they become dependent for support from others. They depend on the labor of others without making any contribution of their own. Whatever problem is encountered, it must be solved by the efforts of others.

The mother is the first influence in the development of her child's occupation interests. Her training during the first four or five years is crucial to the child's orientation towards adult life. Here again early memories can give a clue to a person's possible choice of occupation.

The next step is made by the school, through training the hands, eyes, and ears in their proper functioning. This is particularly important in the training of special subjects.

A child's development is going to be much easier if he or she knows early the occupation they might like to take up later in life. Ask a child what he or she would like to be when they grow up. They will usually give an answer. If a boy says he wants to be a fire fighter or an airplane pilot, he does not really know why he made that choice; but the adult needs to recognize the underlying motive to discover ways in which the striving, that is, what is pushing him forward to the goal, can be made concrete. The goal would represent the way he feels and can achieve superiority; and, from this statement, the adult can discover other opportunities for helping the children to discover a satisfactory goal.

By the age of twelve or fourteen, the choice of occupation should be better fixed. In the healthy adolescent, the strivings for achievement may be greater than the parents' strivings were. For example, Adler noted a child whose father was a policeman and whose own strivings are to be a lawyer or judge. If the father is a teacher, the child's strivings might be to become a university professor.

The games of children often give a hint of the occupation they might wish to enter. For example, a young child who likes to play "school" might very much like to become a teacher. Many children show great mechanical and technical interests when these can be an indication of a later occupation in engineering or some area of science.

Some children develop submissive tendencies and would prefer to be a follower than a leader. This should be discouraged as much as possible for they may end up in a minor position where the work is routine and where all the tasks will be dictated by others. Often sickly children may strive to be doctors, dentists, or pharmacists. Some children well acquainted with death may wish to be ministers.

If the value of money is overstressed in the life of the family, the child will look to future accomplishments only in terms of what money can bring. This can be a great mistake; for when the child reaches adulthood, the emphasis will be only on personal gain and comfort and not on the welfare of the wider community. If the child is only interested in money, he or she will forsake cooperation and look only to personal advantages. If making money is the only goal, no social interest bound up with it. He or she might end up making shady deals or swindling others.

Sometimes an occupation becomes a means of avoiding or evading the problems of life. To become so involved in one's occupation might be a means of avoiding problems of love and marriage. Some might be totally occupied in developing a business that they fail to make friends in their community.

Then, regarding are the problems of unemployment, Adler stressed the need for more schools, especially training schools, technical schools, and adult education. Frequently, the unemployed have never been trained to do any useful work. Some of the great burdens of mankind involve untrained members of society or those not interested in work and the common welfare. The untrained and unskilled account for a disproportionate number of criminals, neurotics, and suicides. All people interested in the future of man's betterment should make efforts to instill in children a better attitude so a greater number of them will enter adulthood where they can take their place in the division of labor.

Too often people cannot make up their minds regarding the choice of an occupation. They vacillate back and forth or are simply too lazy to find work. Adler sees in these people the signs of an inferiority complex.

As with one's relations with society, pampering becomes one of the main contributing conditions to the problem of occupation. As children, the pampered became so dependent that they are unable to strike out on their own.

One of the worst things a parent can do is to force a child into an occupation for which he or she does not have the slightest interest. Usually, this kind of endeavor ends up in complete failure. Adler's daughter, Alexandra Adler, has shown that some people involved in manual labor or in more mental tasks such as accounting or secretarial work may have frequent accidents or make mistakes. This, she maintains is not due to mere chance, but occurs out of attitudes of people who dislike their work. These are errors in the life style (Alexandra Adler, 1941).

LOVE AND MARRIAGE

Regarding a definition of love and marriage, Adler (1931) wrote:

> Love with its fulfilment, marriage, is the most intimate devotion toward a partner of the other sex expressed in physical attraction, comradship and in the decision to have children. It can easily be shown that love and marriage are one side of cooperation—not a cooperation for the welfare of two persons only, but a cooperation also for the welfare of mankind. (p. 262)

Here Adler considered physical attraction to be one of the most important of human strivings. The reason is simple. The chief way to preserve the human race is through propagation. Without physical attraction, propagation will not take place.

If we are able to understand the problems of love and marriage, we will perceive the wider concern for mankind. First, we realize that human beings are divided into two sexes who inhabit the face of the earth. We begin with the cooperation of two individuals. In this instance, each of the two should be more interested in the partner than in himself or herself. If this does not occur, the marriage will not be successful. To have complete devotion, an equality of mutual interests must exist. Neither of the partners must feel subdued or overshadowed. This equality can only be possible if they share the same attitude. Two people cannot live together successfully if one wishes always to be the ruler which the other must obey. The attitude that the man's role is to be a dictator is the reason, according to Adler, for so many divorces. Too frequently today, people have been trained for individual success and not cooperation. The preparation for marriage does not occur overnight. It begins in childhood. Love is a matter of mutual respect to be given and received.

The physical attraction of adults should be fostered in childhood and impressions the child has regarding sympathy and attraction should become evident. These impressions given by the parent of the opposite sex are the beginnings of physical attraction. The boy gains these from his mother, sisters and the girls around him and the girl from her father, brothers and the boys around her. If a child has difficulties with the parent of the opposite sex, later the search for a partner may be for one who will play the subordinate role. Happy marriages do not exist with inequality. For example, if the disagreements between a boy and his mother are very great, his preparation for love and marriage may be hindered and the other sex may be excluded.

Children gain the impression of what marriage is like from observing their parents. If parents are not able to cooperate, this will place a stumbling block in the way of the child's own future marital success.

The worst preparation for marriage is when a parent is always out for his or her own interest. The best preparation is one of cooperation and equality. A good marriage is the best means for bringing up future generations of people of good will.

Regarding the proper characteristics of love partners, Adler wrote (1931, p. 274): "to be faithful and true and trustworthy, not to be reserved, not to be self seeking. . . . It is not even possible to carry through a true comradship if both partners have agreed to pursue their freedom."

As with the problem of pampering as an obstacle in selecting a proper occupation, so too it may be an impediment to successful marriage. Pampered children often feel neglected in marriage. A lack of training for social life may have occurred. A pampered child could be a tyrant in marriage and the partner feels victimized.

Another problem arises in the person who invents a romantic ideal of unobtainable love. Their fictional goal for the perfect partner becomes completely detached from reality. No such perfect person exists.

In other cases, both men and woman have trained themselves to reject their sexual role. This may end up to become the masculine protest. (See pp. 19-22). The rejection of one's sexual role is the explanation Adler gave for frigidity in women and impotence in men.

Another problem in marriage has to do with the children. If parents quarrel and squabble frequently, an unfavorable situation exists for the development of social interest. Some people divorce and marry again and again and still make the same mistakes repeatedly.

A similar mistake is when people get married as a solution to other problems. This is taking a marriage like a mere dose of medicine, which presumably would make both partners well again. But it does not. If your problem is a failure to get along with other people, marriage will not solve it. In marriage one has to get along with the partner.

Adler wrote: "The right solution of the problem of love and marriage belongs to the highest fulfillment of the whole personality. There is no problem more closely involved with happiness and a true and useful expression of life" (1931, p. 284).

Other wrong reasons for getting married include the following:

1. for the sake of economic security,

2. out of pity for the one they married,

3. to secure a servant, and

4. to get oneself out of a particular difficulty, for instance, a jilted lover married to spite the one who jilted him or her.

Some people solve the love problem by avoiding it. For instance, they make such exaggerated demands in their notion of the ideal partner that they can never be fulfilled. The search for the faultless partner will go on endlessly.

Another way of avoiding the love problem is by falling in love with a married man or woman. The love for a married person prevents the development of a free love relationship. Some do it out of lust for power or the pleasure of taking away something that belongs to someone else.

Some men look at love as an adventure without really trying to belong to a single woman. This is the Don Juan type who plays a game of continuous conquests. This is partly true of woman as well. Some lack the ability to enter into a real personal relationship. Underneath, these people suffer from an inferiority complex.

Adler concluded that love is the most beautiful gift bestowed on mankind. In falling in love, the incomprehensible happens. One human being finds another who means everything to him or her, to the exclusion of the rest of the world. Love has taken possession of both partners in the beginning and the two live for each other. Each has the desire to make life more beautiful and richer for the other. Egoism vanishes in the flowering of true love. Each loves the partner more than himself or herself. The highest form of love can be found only in the human race for only humans are capable of putting the well-being of others before themselves (Adler, 1929a).

In conclusion, regarding the right choice for a partner, Adler mentioned the following:

1. intellectual suitability,

2. physical attraction,

3. a capacity to make and retain friendships in general,

4. a greater interest in the partner than oneself,

5. an ability to get along in one's occupation and an interest in it, and

6. an attitude of mutual cooperation.

In his book, *What Life Should Mean To You* (1931), Adler related an old custom used in a certain district of Germany to discover if an engaged couple is properly prepared for marriage. The two partners are given a double-handled saw. Each is given one end and they are asked to saw the trunk of a tree while the villagers and relatives stand around to watch. If trust does not exist between the two, they will tug against each other and nothing will be accomplished. If one of them takes the lead and does the entire task while the other gives way, the task will take twice as long. Ideally, each will work equally hard in mutual cooperation to complete the task so their combined efforts will result in mutual cooperation.

Adler found he could discover the style of life in other ways as well as certain problems involved in it. The inevitable problems of life and sometimes their solutions can be found in an examination of dreams which is the subject of the next chapter.

IMPLICATIONS

Adler identified three areas of human relations which he identified as the "Three Problems of Life." In each case the solutions involve the fulfillment of social interest. A lack of social interest will tend to create and magnify these problems. The three areas include (1) our relationships with society, (2) our work, and (3) love and marriage.

The one thing that binds us all together is that we are all members of the human race. Life would be very difficult if each of us chose to live and work by ourselves. Cooperation with others is the key to survival. Furthermore, pampering is one of the main obstacles to successful relationships with others. The pampered child grows up to live only for himself or herself, thus obstructing genuine social relationships.

A second problem of utmost importance is choosing the right occupation. In helping a person find or choose the most appropriate occupation, the parents can be of assistance. Adler warns against using a job as a means of avoiding other people. He further stressed the overvaluing of money as a means for achieving success. Since we spend a good part of our lives in our work, our occupation should be one we enjoy doing, not only for the work itself but also for the people with whom we must interact.

An important procedure is for us to decide either in high school or college the occupation we wish to pursue. Here vocational guidance on the part of the family and the schools will be helpful. We must learn a trade or an occupation. If one has set up proper future goals during the developmental years, the choice should not be too difficult. Our work is one of the ways we can fulfill our strivings for superiority.

The third area is love and marriage. Choosing a mate can be one of the most rewarding experiences of our lives. If we choose the wrong partner, the results can be devastating. Marriage should lead to the highest fulfillment of human happiness. Alder warns us against merely marrying for security, or out of pity, or simply to find a servant.

Marriage should involve mutual attraction, intellectual compatibility, a fulfilling concern for the other person, an attitude of mutual cooperation and a capacity for love and friendship.

DREAMS AND THEIR INTERPRETATION

Adler pointed out that from earliest times man has been trying to find out the significance of dreams. In Egyptian, Greek, and Roman times enormous importance was attached to dreams. In the Old Testament, we read of the prophecies revealed in dreams.

Adler had read Freud's *Interpretation of Dreams* (1900) shortly after its publication and was much impressed by it. As time passed and Adler broke from Freud to develop his own Individual Psychology, he differed from Freud in many respects with regard to the interpretation of dreams. In one respect, at least, he agreed with Freud—that is, dreams tell us something important about the person and any psychology that ignores dreams as part of its explanation is incomplete.

In other respects, Adler was critical of Freud's analysis of dreams. First of all, because every person is a unique individual, for Adler no universal or fixed symbols are in dreams as Freud had suggested, i.e., long, pointed, objects symbolize the male sex organs and enclosures the female genitalia. For Adler, each dream must be interpreted in the light of the individual personality doing the dreaming. One should never interpret isolated dreams. Dreams should only be interpreted in relation to the dreamer and with the situation in which the dreamer finds himself or herself at the time of the dream. Secondly, Adler objected to Freud's emphasis on so many sex symbols. Furthermore, dreams were not disguises, but expressions of an individual's personality and his or her way of dealing with life.

For Adler, dreams were part of the mind's creative activity. If we can discover what one expects in a dream, we shall come very close to discovering the purpose of the dream. The function of the dream is to meet the difficulties with which we are confronted in our daily lives and, hopefully, to provide a solution. The purpose of the dream is to support the style of life against demands of common sense. Suppose a person's goal is to have a lot of money. Common sense tells us that to acquire a large fortune, one must work very hard and struggle for it. An easier way would be to gamble and win it. The dream serves the same function. Dreaming is the adversary of common sense. The dream is an attempt to make a bridge between an individual's style of life and his or her present problems without making any new demands on the style of life. In the dream we select those images that fit in with the style of life and express what the style of life demands. To meet the difficulties realistically would call for common sense, but, in those instances, the style of life refuses to give way.

In order to understand the dream we must first consider sleep. Sleep gives us rest and recuperation. It also brings the physical and psychological activities nearer to a state of relaxation.

Psychological life persists during sleep. What Freud called the dream censor is nothing more than a greater distance from reality which pervades during sleep.

The unintelligibility of the dream is not a matter of chance. The same unintelligibility is seen in waking life when a person wishes to defend his mistakes with far-fetched arguments.

To set down strict rules for dream interpretation is impossible. The dream tells us nothing more than we could find in other forms of psychological experience.

Dreams represent another way in which a person can express his or her style of life. They may be forward looking and act as a bridge between the current situation of the dream and the future goals.

In dreaming, consciousness and unconsciousness become united. This notion is in direct contrast to Freud's distinction in which he believed the dreams were the expression of the unconscious. Likewise, in stressing the forward-looking nature of dreams, Adler was opposing the Freudian notion of dreams being expressions of old, repressed conflicts.

Another possible function of the dream is that of problem solving. Through the dream, we may consider possible courses of attacking our problems. In this sense, they may be useful in psychotherapy because they may bring problems to the surface. In particular, they represent an individual's particular goals in accordance with his or her unique style of life. Here they may present glimpses to the future. They may present solutions to problems of life. Adler generally rejected Freud's notion that dreams were the expression of unfulfilled wishes. In being forward looking, dreams can provide clues to future goals.

Since dreams are one way of expressing the style of life, here we can find the prototype of any person's life style. For example, many people are basically cowardly. In this instance, one would presume that these people would have many dreams of fear, anxiety and danger. The presumption turns out to be correct. Anxious people have anxious dreams.

Adler mentioned the case of a young man who tended to be a quitter. When faced with an examination, he worried the entire day and finally said to himself, "There is not enough time." That night, he dreamt of falling. Adler pointed out that such a dream was inevitable because his life style was to avoid the problems of life. One means of which was to quit when things become too tough. Dreams of falling frequently represent inferiority and of low self-esteem.

Adler also cited another case of a student who behaved in the opposite way. He made progress in his studies and was not afraid of work. Faced with a similar examination, this young man dreamed that he climbed the highest mountain and was enriched by the mountain air (Adler, 1931).

Adler also cited the case of the student with limited ability. This person can only go so far. In some instances, he cannot surmount the difficulties in life. He dreams of being hunted or chased.

Even though dreams are often future oriented, Adler denied that they have any prophetic aspect. Suppose you dream that a person dies and in six months that person does actually die. This is nothing more than what a physician or close relative would foresee. The person did not appear well. Most dreams that appear prophetic are based on evidence that certain events will actually take place at some future time.

Dreams often convey feelings and emotions about a situation. Adler cited the following case. A married man was not content with his family life. He had two children but was concerned that his wife did not care for them properly. One night he dreamed he had a third child who got lost and could not be found. In his dream, he blamed his wife. Adler's interpretation was that he was not courageous enough to allow in the dream one of his two sons to get lost so he invented the third child. Also, he thought his wife was overburdened by taking care of the two children, so he invented in his dream a third child who would perish. In this dream, the man created a strong emotion against the wife. Here the man's style of life is dominated by defeat and thoughts of death. The dream also was dominated by the wife's neglect of the children.

A husband who was the father of two children quarrelled constantly with his wife. He was aware that his wife had not married him for love. As a child he was spoiled but later was dethroned by a younger brother. His relationship with his wife was a mixture of opposites. Sometimes he was patient and affectionate. At other times, he would have outbursts of fury. He also doted on his two sons and they responded accordingly. His wife could not match the affection he showered on the two boys. The man interpreted this as neglect. The situation continued with each spouse experiencing a lack of respect and affection for the other. One night the husband dreamed of bleeding female bodies that were being flung about in the air. Adler's interpretation was that the man had reached his wit's end as far as his wife was concerned and did not care to have any further confrontation with her.

A college professor worked under a dean whom he and many of his colleagues felt was ineffective and incompetent. One day, an announcement was made that the dean was taking a year's leave of absence. That night the professor dreamed that he had been appointed to take the dean's place. The professor felt that despite his own inexperience in administrative matters, he would do a far better job than the ineffective dean was doing.

COMMON DREAM ELEMENTS

Adler rejected Freud's notion that some dream symbols were fixed and universal for everyone. Dreams must always be interpreted individually in the light of what one knows about the person. However, Adler found that certain dream elements occurred with considerable frequency; for example, dreams of flying, falling, being chased, and so forth. Although not to be interpreted as universal, Adler found a certain similarity of meanings. Furthermore, one cannot explain the meaning of a dream without a full knowledge of that individual's personality. Despite the fact that no strict rules of dream interpretation can be identified, Adler did suggest some possibilities that might occur frequently and mean the same thing for more than one person.

Dreams of falling are very common, particularly among neurotics and may represent the fear of loss of prestige, security, or status.

Dreams of flying are also very common and may express a mood of bouyancy and courage. They may represent the overcoming of difficulties and the striving for the goal of superiority.

Dreams of paralysis often represent a warning that current problems are insoluble.

Dreams of examinations can refer to an unpreparedness or an inability to face the problem before a person.

Dreams about death may indicate that one is still concerned with or under the influence of a dead person.

Dreams of missing a train (or bus or plane, etc.) mean that one has escaped defeat by arriving too late.

Dreams of being improperly clothed (walking down the street in one's pajamas, underwear, etc.) may indicate a fear of being detected concerning some fault, impropriety, or imperfection.

Dreams of being pursued by animals or monsters may indicate feelings of inferiority.

Dreams of cruelty in which the dreamer takes an active part indicate a strong desire for revenge.

Recurring dreams are excellent indicators of the style of life. They give an indication of how one is attempting to achieve the goal of superiority.

The following example from Ansbacher (1977) serves as an excellent example of the whole approach to the matter of Adlerian dream interpretation.

William D. Dement, dream physiologist, reported the following: "One subject in our laboratory, in a single night, ran the gamut from being with two hippotamuses in a mill pond, through a taffy pull at the Soviet Embassy, to hearing Handel's Messiah sung by a thousand voice choir in a beautiful cathedral and back to writing at his desk" (p. 66).

Dement gave this as an example of the widely unpredictable nature of dream content. Ansbacher replied to this by saying that although the dream content might be unpredictable, the creativity of the dream is clear. The common denominator is bigness, strength, activity and a pleasant-feeling tone. From these denominators can be inferred that during the dreamer's waking life great activity, bouyancy, and optimism occur with some grandiosity and manic traits. This is also a cultured person, interested in music. When this interpretation was given to Dement, he replied, "The individual in question is exactly as you described him" (p. 66).

We may conclude, then, that the dream is another way of discovering a person's style of life. Dreams are creative, may give us an indication of our problems and possible ways of solving them and can be an expression of our emotions, and an indication of our goals and future strivings.

However, dreams are not the only way of discovering the style of life. The same information may be found in other sources, such as early memories (see pp. 61-63), bodily movements, and day dreams. Adler does not make the distinction between night dreams and day dreams that Freud did. In fact, if you were asked to relate a dream and you could not think of one, so you made one up (fantasy), this would tell just as much as if you had related a real dream.

With regard to the forward-looking nature of dreams, Adler (1933) referred to a dream of the Greek poet, Simonides. He was about to undertake a sea journey but dreamed that the ghost of a dead man warned him against taking the forthcoming sea voyage. Simonides remained home and the ship he was to take sank in a storm and all aboard were lost. Adler does not interpret this dream as prophetic, but merely an indication that the poet did not want to take the trip, since travel by sea in those days was dangerous. The dream created a strong emotion that made it possible for him to follow his real inclination of remaining home. The actual disaster was coincidental and merely indicated that Simonides had made an accurate prediction of what was to happen.

IMPLICATIONS

Like other psychodynamic theorists such as Freud and Jung, Adler stressed the importance of dreams. Through our dreams we make a bridge between our style of life and can give insight into our future goals. At other times dreams are expressions of our emotions. A man who had aspirations for future financial security dreamed he had bought a twenty room mansion with many servants. A woman who had difficulty getting along with men and had gone through two divorces dreamed men were pursuing her with ball bats.

Adler rejected the Freudian notion of fixed or universal symbols in dreams. In order to understand the true meaning of a dream one must have a full understanding of the personality of the dreamer. To the degree that we have some insight into ourselves it is possible that we can understand the true significance of our dreams.

Recurrent dreams are of particular importance. An aging man frequently dreams of his youth when he was carefree and unburdened with the problems of age. A woman who never completed college dreams she is back in the classroom trying to finish her work.

An analysis of the dream can give us understanding of our style of life, our future, unfilled desires, or our prevailing feelings about others.

SAFE-GUARDING TENDENCIES

Part of the strivings for superiority is a need for self esteem. When our self esteem is threatened we may attempt some technique to protect ourselves from such threats. These devices are aimed at protecting the self and maintaining the already established style of life.

In many ways, the safe-guarding tendencies bear a similarity to Freud's mechanisms of defense. For both Adler and Freud, these tendencies were attempts to protect the ego.

However, some basic differences do exist between the two conceptions. Freud's defense mechanisms were attempts to protect the ego from anxiety which he interpreted always as a conscious, unpleasant experience derived, ordinarily, from threats originating in the unconscious. For Adler, the safe-guarding tendencies operated as protections against external (outside) demands placed upon the person.

For Freud, the defense mechanisms were to be found in everyone and a person got into trouble only when the defenses became exaggerated and dominated the personality. For Adler, the safe-guarding tendencies could occur in both normal and abnormal people, but he placed more emphasis on their operation in neurotic individuals. In any event, since Adler did allow that safe-guarding tendencies can occur in normal people, we shall discuss them first and in the following chapter deal exclusively with the development of neurotic behavior.

Finally, Freud believed that the defense mechanisms operated at the unconscious level, for if we were conscious of the fact that we were engaging in defensive activities such as rationalization or projection, for example, Freud maintained that the defenses would fail to work. Since Adler did not make a clear distinction between consciousness and unconsciousness, the safe-guarding tendencies could operate at either level.

For Adler, one of the problems that neurotics experience is that their own strivings for personal superiority may appear to others as ridiculous and foolish. A discovery of this would lead to considerable embarrassment. To counteract this fear which is really a fiction, neurotics construct the safe-guarding devices to protect themselves from the emergence of the inferiority complex which characterizes all neurotics.

EXCUSES

The behavior of neurotics is an attempt to avoid difficult problems of life. In building up a barrier, a person is protected and feels more comfortable and secure. Excuses can be of two kinds: the "Yes, but" and the "If, only" types. In the "Yes, but," a person states what he or she would like to do which sounds very good and positive; then follows the excuse as a safeguard. Consider the following example. A college student states that he would like to make an A on his examination, *but* he has two other tests the same day and only so many hours are in the day in which to study; or, the housewife states that she would like to participate in a charitable enterprise, *but* her cleaning woman just quit and she had to do all the housework herself; or, the professor says he would like to engage in research, *but* he has so many students and papers to grade that he has no time. The real fact of the matter is that he is lazy and cares nothing about research, but to admit that would be an excessive threat to his self esteem.

In the "If, only" excuses, the statements are phrased in a different way. "If only I had a college education, I would not be stuck in this mediocre job," or "If only I had better looking clothes, I would have been asked to join the fraternity," or "If only I had gone to prep school, I would have been accepted at

enhance the self by depreciating the environment. This tendency may have arisen in childhood when the child's desire was to hurt the parents or gain their attention. To injure another person through hurting oneself is one of the most subtle techniques of self-enhancement. Adler cited the case of a woman who hurt her husband by confessing an earlier incident of infidelity. Although she appeared to experience great guilt feelings, she really wanted her husband to suffer.

Although self-accusation appears to be the opposite of depreciation, both are attempts at expressing personal superiority. Through the depreciation of the self, one undervalues another person's making oneself look good by comparison. Although a person inflicts pain on himself, the ultimate purpose is to hurt the other person again to protect one's self esteem.

DISTANCE

Distance is a category of safe-guarding tendencies in which a person attempts to "escape" a problem by setting up a distance between the self and the problem. Adler identified four modes of distance: *moving backward, standing still, hesitation,* and *constructing obstacles.*

Moving Backward

Here, Adler's reference is to any tendency to protect one's self esteem by reverting to an earlier and more secure period in one's life. This tendency has its counterpart in Freud's defense mechanism of *regression* which means reverting backward behaviorally to a period in life when fewer problems and fewer threats existed to the self. However, a distinction needs to be made. In the Freudian concept, the defense operates unconsciously and includes the suppression of earlier painful experiences. Adler's concept of moving backward may be considered as attempts to protect the inflated goal of superiority. Moving backwards can be expressed in attempts at suicide, fainting, most phobias, compulsions, anorexia, amnesia, drug and alcohol addiction, criminal tendencies, and anxiety attacks. The mechanism behind all these symptoms is to gain attention from others in order to get some control over them.

Children like to gain attention. Certainly suicide attempts, fainting, failure to eat (anorexia) are clear examples of attention-getting devices which draw concern from other people so regarding their well being. Likewise, these symptoms attract sympathy which bolsters self esteem. Going backwards, likewise, involves less responsible behavior. We can not expect the responsibility of children to be the same as that of adults. Alcohol and drug addiction can be interpreted as examples of that irresponsible behavior.

Standing Still

This safe-guarding device closely resembles the Freudian defense of *fixation*. It differs in much the same way as moving backwards in that it may be partly conscious. Instead of protecting the ego from anxiety (Freud), it safeguards the ego by giving an inflated feeling of superiority. In standing still, one avoids the threats of failure. Adler likened it to a witches circle which has been drawn around a person. This prevents him or her from moving closer to the realities of life, from facing the truth, from taking a stand or from making a decision. Sometimes in doing nothing (standing still), problems may solve themselves. One can always make great promises of what he or she is going to do, but, in standing still, one's self esteem is preserved by never starting the task. Moving ahead to the next step will not be a threat. Consider a man who never marries. By standing still, in his bachelorhood his self esteem cannot be threatened by being turned down by a woman in a marriage proposal.

Hesitation

Adler referred to it as "hesitation and back and forth." Here the distance is secured. This device is aimed at wasting time. Hand-washing compulsions, retracing one's steps, destroying work already completed, leaving work unfinished, arriving too late, or being unable to make up one's mind are all examples of hesitation.

When faced with a problem, a person vacillates or stalls, figuring all possibilities from several viewpoints, but nothing is accomplished; but, from an individual's point of view, a failure to act can protect one's self esteem.

Hesitation bears a close relationship to standing still except that in standing still a decision is completely prevented. The safe-guarding aspect of hesitation can be seen in the fiction which begins with "if." "If I had a louder voice, I could be a great actor." Usually the "if" clause contains an unfulfillable difficulty which only the person can change.

Constructing Obstacles

This is probably the least severe of the safe-guarding devices under the general heading of distance. The obstacle can be likened to a straw man which can be easily knocked down. The self esteem can be protected because the symptoms are not so severe that they cannot be overcome. Symptoms may include fatigue, insomnia, constipation, intestinal disorders, or headaches. In these symptoms, the individual puts himself or herself to the test of whether he or she is able to overcome the obstacle.

EXCLUSION TENDENCIES

These constitute a later version of Adler's concept of distance. As a safeguard, an individual erects a wall against the demands of living in a social community. This constitutes a withdrawal from the world as a means of avoiding or escaping one's problems. In Adler's words, "He tries to keep at a distance the real confronting problem of life and confines himself to circumstances in which he feels able to dominate. In this way, he builds for himself a narrow stable, closes the door, and spends his life away from the wind, the sunlight, and the fresh air" (Adler, 1956, p. 278). In short, the individual becomes inaccessible to the behavior of other people. This kind of insulation can actually be physical where one becomes a recluse, a hermit, or it can merely be psychological where one is in the midst of people but fails to interact with them.

With the exclusive tendencies we conclude our discussion of the safe-guarding devices. They are found in all people, but, when they become predominant patterns in the personality, they become expressions of neurotic behavior. They are intended to protect a person from failure. Adler placed their origin in the inferiority complex. They are intended to combat inferiority feelings, but, unfortunately, they end up being self-defeating. As attempts to protect one's self esteem they end up as expressions of self interest and self centeredness. There is no consideration of the possibility that self esteem would be better preserved if self centeredness were given up in favor of genuine social interest.

IMPLICATIONS

In many ways, Adler's safe-guarding devices resemble Freud's mechanisms of defense. They are techniques we use to bolster up or protect our self esteem. These are not proper solutions to life's problems, rather they are techniques to by pass or ward off certain difficulties. When used in excess they may create more problems. Since Adler did not separate consciousness from unconsciousness, their use can be recognized. Also we can identify when we are engaging in these protective devices.

If we recognize them, we will be better able to confront the real problem in order to find more adequate solutions.

Making **excuses** for our inadequacies or failures stands high on the list of safe-guarding devices. First is the "yes, but" type of excuse. "Yes, I would like to join you at the party, but I have scads of work to do." The fact of the matter is that I really do not want to go because it will be a boring experience. Then another type of excuse is the "if only." This will soften the blow of inadequacy. "If only I were ten years younger, I could take that job." Here again I didn't want the job.

Under the general heading of **aggression** we find the use of **depreciation** of other people. By belittling other people we place ourselves in a more favorable light. "I don't know how you got elected president of the club. You have absolutely no experience."

Accusation or blaming others is a second form of aggression. "It's your fault the car broke down. You never bothered to have it checked out before we went on the trip." "We missed the train because you took so long to get ready."

Under the general heading of **distance,** Adler refers to **moving backwards.** Here we revert to some early period in our development where fewer threats to sour self esteem were present, and we have fewer responsibilities. "I wish you would quit acting so childish and face up to your responsibilities: the things expected of you." This is similar to Freudian "regression."

In **standing still** we go so far in our development and stop. This is equivalent to the Freudian mechanism of fixation. "When are you going to grow up and find a girl to marry?"

Hesitation involves vacillation or stalling. "If we fiddle around long enough, maybe the problem will solve itself." If we can't make up our minds, we won't make the wrong decision.

Sometimes we create obstacles which impede our progression. These are the straw people who interfere with our development. These often take the form of physical symptoms. "I can't join you tonight. I have a splitting headache."

Exclusive tendencies completes the list of safe-guarding devices. In this tendency a person might remove himself or herself from society at large and become a hermit or a recluse. In other cases a person insulates himself or herself psychological and becomes a difficult person with whom to communicate. "You can't carry on a conversation with him. He never says anything. Just a silent Sam."

THE NEUROTIC CHARACTER

Adler agreed with Freud and Jung that abnormal and normal behavior differed in degree, not kind. The well adjusted or normal individual goes about meeting life's challenges in a successful way. Good adjustment involves an obligation to interact appropriately in three areas where life's problems will arise: work, society, and sex and love. Social interest is, of course, a requisite for successful social living. Almost all maladjusted individuals lack social interest. In Chapter XII, we shall deal specifically with the criminal personality where either social interest is minimal or completely lacking. In this chapter we shall limit ourselves to Adler's conception of the neurotic personality or character. Neurotics accounted for the largest number of cases that Adler treated.

Freud had seen the neurotic condition as arising out of intrapsychic conflict, that is, between the structures of the mental apparatus: the super ego, the ego, and the id. In Adler's holistic conception of personality, such a distinction between parts of the personality was impossible. Thus, even in mental disorders, a dynamic unity existed.

ORIGINS

The mistakes in life, that is, what Adler considered the neurotics, arose out of failures to solves life's problems. Among other things, these failures resulted from a lack of cooperation and social interest. Since all of us fail at times in cooperation and do not always express social interest for our fellow men, differences are again one of degree (Adler, 1926).

In the *Neurotic Constitution* (1926), Adler mentioned the following conditions from which neurotic behavior originates:

1. inferiority feelings in childhood;

2. inappropriate uses of safe-guarding devices (see previous chapter);

3. inappropriate and inadequate compensations for inferiority feelings;

4. a fictional goal of superiority centered entirely around oneself;

5. inappropriate methods, feelings, and attitudes which lead to exaggerated and fictitious self enhancement; and

6. failure to develop one's potential social interest and cooperation.

SUPPORTING FACTORS

Certain supporting factors are also going to be handled successfully by normal individuals, however, within the neurotic condition, something goes wrong. What also should be mentioned at this juncture is that the neurotic condition begins early in childhood and operates in the gradual development of a faulty style of life.

Organ Inferiority

Adler began his exposition of the neurotic condition with a discussion of organ inferiority. Proper compensation must be made for inferior organs. In some instances, a child with deficient vision may concentrate on colors and lines, but he or she may be so deficient in vision that such attention is mocked by other children. Because of this failure to see like other children, the visually handicapped child gives up and may become excessively aggressive. In other cases, the constitutionally inferior child may construct a goal of selfish personal enhancement, instead of a more realistic striving for superiority. Those children with organ inferiorities may direct their aggression towards their parents.

Adler quoted a fictitious child to make his point (Adler, 1926, p. 58), "The fault lies with my parents, with my lot, because I'm the youngest, because I was born too late, because I am a Cinderella, perhaps, because I am not the child of these parents, of this father, of this mother, because I am too small, too weak, have too small a head, am too homely . . ."

Accordingly the tendency to exaggerate and emphasize existing defects plays an important role in the development of the neuroses.

Pampering

In Chapter VI, we discussed pampering as one of the conditions contributing to a faulty style of life. The life style of each neurotic is different. Frequently, when a pampered child tries out a certain method and finds it successful, he or she will try again. If a certain neurotic symptom is selected in childhood and found successful in adulthood, the neurotic will try it again as a means of furthering his or her strivings. Examples would include childhood bullying or whining, which later appear successful. If one method is not successful, he or she may try another. In any case, the goal is the same, to achieve a feeling of superiority without working to improve the general situation. A discouraged child may find that tears bring attention so the child becomes a cry baby. Tears and complaints become extremely useful weapons in reducing others to slavery. Part of pampering involves giving in to such methods in childhood by getting one's own way.

In one way or other, Adler maintained, all neurotics have a pampered style of life. Even if they were not pampered as children, in adulthood they find themselves in a situation similar to the pampered child. This is their life attitude. They may have been neglected as children, so as adults they pamper themselves. They are caught between a fear of failure and a desire for success. Their growing sense of inferiority forces the neurotics to deal with rebuffs which appear to reinforce their hostility. Their attitude toward the environment becomes one of mild aggression, and they use it to fight. Although they fight against the possibilities of defeat and self-destruction, their hostility towards the environment persists, but the hostility prevents them from finding a path which might lead to success. Or, through their failures, they may withdraw from situations of responsibility and are drawn to make excuses and alibies. They will exaggerate their weakness and mysterious pains in order to say "I told you so." Common sense tells us that in order to reach a goal, one must persist in an orderly fashion, but the neurotics will take the easy solutions and shortcuts. Adler stressed the fact that neurotic symptoms come from these early preparatory techniques which were found to be useful in achieving personal superiority.

Oversensitivity

Adler maintained that oversensitivity was found equally in all neurotics. Most patients readily admit that they are easily hurt by words or facial expressions of others. If the neurotic denies his or her sensitivity, the fact that it exists can easily be verified by close relatives. This has its origin in childhood when the boy or girl complained of being used, neglected, hurt, small, disparaged, or unfavored. In the most extreme form, it can take on the veil of a delusion: "You are all plotting against me." Sometimes the person attributes his or her misfortune to "bad luck." Also possibly oversensitive adults may have been the victims of frequent accidents, delays, failures, or discouragements. The oversensitive adult was typically a selfish child.

Aversive Experiences

Every neurotic has been trained from childhood to retreat from tasks that he or she might fear, through failing them, or injure his faulty personal striving for superiority. The striving lacks any social interest. The possibility of continued threats of defeat exists, as if he or she were living in a hostile country. As a result of already established impatience and greed, conflicts will arise that ordinarily are not necessary. These aversive experiences make a retreat easier which already has been set by a faulty style of life. Had a person developed some degree of social interest, the trauma would have been less threatening. The trauma is not the sole cause of the difficulty. It only enhances a problem that already had been established by a faulty style of life. For Adler, therapy was not intended to unearth the trauma and strengthen the ego, as in Freudian analysis, but to bring forth insight into the reorganization of the striving forces within the personality.

Shock Effects

Life itself involves problems which demand a social solution. The person who has not been prepared early in life to confront these problems may resort to neurotic symptoms. The difficulties do not lie in problems themselves but in an inability to cope with them. For instance, the problem might be a disappointment in a love relationship. Few people have not experienced a shock from such a situation. The disappointment itself need not cause a neurotic condition. The difficulty lies only, if the condition persists, in many disappointments in love. In this case, the individual will begin to avoid all intimate personal relationships. The person may become shy and embarrassed and manifest psychosomatic symptoms such as heart palpitations, perspiration, or symptoms of stomach distress. The difficulty lies ultimately in an insufficiently developed social feeling for others. Adler gave the example of a person who loses money in a business venture and feels a shock from the loss. The shock itself does not lead to the neurosis. The person becomes neurotic only when he or she remains in the state of shock and does nothing to overcome it. The implication for the neurosis, in this instance, is that the person has never acquired a sufficient degree of cooperation and only if he or she is guaranteed success in the next venture will the shock effects disappear. When the person is unprepared for the tasks of life, which means that he or she has never learned to be a co-worker from his childhood, the shock effects will become permanent. The neurotic safeguards himself or herself through the symptoms. They are the unknowing explanation of the effects of the shock. The safeguards become a safeguard against losing their self-esteem, which has already been tempted in childhood, usually by being pampered (Adler, 1929b).

Sexual Factors

Although Adler did not stress sexual factors in the neuroses as Freud did, he did allow for some "typical occasions for the onset of the neuroses" which were sexual in nature. These were first described in his book, *The Neurotic Constitution* (1921).

Such sexual factors include: (1) uncertainty regarding one's sexual role, (2) onset of menstruation, (3) the time of sexual intercourse, (4) marriage, (5) pregnancy, (6) childbirth, (7) diminuation of potency in aging, and (8) loss of a loved one. All these conditions call for the intensification of preparatory attitudes toward life. The bond that ties these conditions together is the expectation of a new social reality for which the neurotic character is not sufficiently prepared due to a lack of social interest. These conditions allow for new struggles and new dangers. These result in an intensification of the safe-guarding tendencies, the most extreme being suicide. These events intensify a neurotic readiness, precipitated by an already present egotism and lack of social feeling.

Inferiority and Superiority Complexes

In Chapter II, we discussed inferiority and superiority complexes as the extension of normal inferiority feelings. When inferiority feelings become so intense, they are designated as inferiority complexes. When the inferiority feelings reach such an intense degree, Adler wrote,

> Every neurotic has an inferiority complex. No neurotic is distinguished from other neurotics by the fact that he has an inferiority complex and the others have none. He is distinguished from the others by the kind of situation in which he feels unable to continue on the useful side of life by the limits he has put on his strivings and activities. (Adler, 1929b, p. 71)

The inferiority complex manifests itself in an individual when he or she is unable to solve existing problems in a socially useful way. On the other hand, the neurotic's evasion of the problems of life may take the form of a superiority complex. This involves the false belief that the person is above or better than others. Through it, the individual sets up unrealistic and fantastic goals which will only result in failure and the intensification of the inferiority complex. "It is as if the sufferer were in a trap and the more he struggles the worse his position becomes" (Adler, 1931, p. 146).

The person with a superiority complex uses it as a method of escape from life's difficulties. He or she believes that they are superior when they are not, so the delusion of superiority becomes a compensation for the intense state of inferiority, which becomes unbearable.

The superiority complex should not be confused with normal strivings for superiority. The normal strivings are expressed in an ambition to be successful in work and other activities of life. Normal strivings involve social interest so one's own strivings for betterment become integrated with a general uplift of the group. The superiority complex expresses itself in exaggerated demands on one's self. It expresses itself in vanity and disdain for others.

ANXIETY DISORDERS

All abnormal behavior is viewed by Adler as serious errors in living. Anxiety disorders typically express themselves in a fear of defeat. Phobias, in particular, block the way to further activity. In particular, agoraphobia (fear of open places) can be an expression of a fear of hostile persecution. When this phobia reaches the point where one is afraid to leave the house, the neurotic imposes his or her demands on others. Everyone must come to see them. In Adler's interpretation, the individual becomes the king who dominates others (Adler, 1931). The agoraphobic loses the fear or anxiety when he or she remains at home to dominate others. This attitude of dominance typifies all neurotics who exclude that part of their lives in which they do not feel strong enough to conquer others.

Anxiety is a subjective experience for an uncompensated inferiority feeling. It develops when the neurotic's conflict with the environment increases and the possibility of defeat is enhanced. Typically, the action in which anxiety is designed to imitate is to retreat from the threatening situation. In a background of anxiety, the neurotic can go forward to construct whatever symptoms the nature of the situation may require. Anxiety develops out of the fear that one's fictional goal may be contradicted. When the fiction is threatened with collapse, anxiety begins to mount.

Adler (1931) cited the case of a married woman who had attacks of anxiety when her husband was late in coming home from work. She was accustomed to being overindulged by her husband. When his business obligations prevented him from devoting so much of his attention to her, she felt that she was being excluded. By developing the anxiety attacks, she interfered with her husband's business to become master of the situation.

COMPULSIVE AND OBSESSIVE REACTIONS

The compulsive neurotic places a distance between himself or herself and the necessity of making decisions. Instead of solving a problem, the compulsive neurotic uses up all of his or her energy in the compulsive activities instead of devoting them to solving the basic problems of life. Adler likened these people to a Don Quixote who fights wind mills. They concern themselves with matters (handwashing, touching, cleaning) which accomplish little which is socially useful. Their activities only serve to waste time. For them, time becomes a dangerous foe which would impel them to solve life's problems, conditions with which they are unable to cope.

Frequently, compulsive activities are expressions of hostility. The time-wasting behavior can serve as an annoyance to those they dislike. A compulsive housewife who spends the day scrubbing the house can torment her husband who is required to spend his evenings in the kitchen so the rest of the house will not be mussed up. The compulsive neurotic is able to sidestep real, but difficult, problems by confusing them with simpler, repetitious tasks.

INSOMNIA

Adler maintained that people who cannot sleep have a purpose which is supported by not sleeping. Another person always will be involved. So the insomnia only becomes an effective means of attacking that persons. Married women use their sleeplessness to attack their husbands and vice-versa. Sometimes insomnia is an expression of thwarted ambition. If the person could only sleep, he or she could accomplish much more in waking life. However, should the person be able to sleep, as to whether any more would be accomplished is doubtful. The ambition is merely a facade. The amount of sleep and the degree of accomplishment are entirely unrelated.

CONVERSION REACTIONS

Conversion reactions are substitutes for anxiety. In Adler's day and prior to 1980, these reactions were identified as hysteria. However, in 1980, the American Psychiatric Association in DSM III (*Diagnostic and Statistical Manual*, third edition) dropped the term, hysteria. Whatever the name, the conversion reactions take many forms. Adler considered "hysterical convulsions" (fits) to be a good example of the conversion of a psychic (psychological) feeling into a motor reaction. These psychological convulsions, in the adult, have their prototype in a child's rigidity and negativism. Then, also the nervous twitchings, tics, and tremors operate as means of gaining attention. These reactions will tend to center around an organ which is weak or was weak in childhood.

Closely related to the conversion reactions are the dissociative reactions, which operate as a departure from the logic of the environment. They reveal a lack of contact with reality. In extreme cases, they take the form of amnesia, fugues (wandering away), or the multiple personality. In these instances, the person "turns over a new leaf" and assumes a different existence when dissatisfied with the old one. Through the conversion and dissociative reactions a person fulfills the "as if" principle.

MELANCHOLIA (Depression)

Melancholia develops in persons who in early childhood developed a style of life dependent on achievements and supports from other people. The people always try to lean on others and do not mind hinting at their own inadequacy and need to submit to others. In difficulties they evade the main issue. Life becomes a great hazard. As children they had low self esteem. They were readily willing to take all the blame for all failures and errors. Their inward manifestation of blame is really an expression of their own aggression towards their environment. The aggressive nature of melancholia is seen in the occasional murder impulse. Their weapons of aggression are complaints and tears through which they show their weakness and need for help.

The melancholic attempts to achieve the goal of superiority by taking detours. Adler suggested that this was done through the payment of a price, their depression. He called this the "melancholic fiction."

SUICIDE

Individual Psychology maintains that every individual is directed towards the successful solution of each problem of life as one encounters that problem throughout the life span. Success in problem solving is, however, somewhat of a subjective matter. Suicide is a solution to a problem or possibly many problems of life, which occur when a person has arrived at the end of a limited social interest.

As children, suicidal people were poor losers. Even though they never made a direct attack against others, they expressed a style of life which attempted to influence others through chronic complaining and suffering. They tended to collapse under psychological stress when confronted with difficult life situations. All this occurred in a background of their own ambitions and vanity. Through pampering they over-valued their own self opinion. The lifestyle of a potential suicide is characterized by hurting others through belittling himself or herself.

Adler cited the case of a pampered young man, unable to overcome tremendous difficulties at school, who committed suicide. He left a suicide note to his sister. "Don't tell mother

what I have done. Her present address is _____
_____ . Tell her when she
comes back that I no longer had any enjoyment in life. Tell her
to put flowers on my grave every day" (Adler, 1933, pp. 133-134).
This illustrates Adler's usual interpretation that suicide is a
revenge against someone else. Also, the suicide has been
precipitated by insurmountable difficulties as the individual
perceives them.

Other forms of psychological difficulties have been discussed in previous chapters, for example, problems involved
with work and sex were discussed in Chapter VII. Problems of
crime and delinquency will be discussed in Chapter XII.
Because Adler was primarily a practitioner, his methods of
treatment for these psychological difficulties will be discussed
in the following chapter.

IMPLICATIONS

The neurotics constitute a group of people who have failed
to solve life's problems. In most instances they lack social
interest along with other deviant groups such as criminals.
Adler identified the neurotics as people (1) with strong
inferiority feelings stemming from childhood, (2) inappropriate
use of safe-guarding devices, (3) a fictional goal centered solely
around themselves, (4) and a failure to develop social interest.
The neurotic has developed a faulty style of life based on
inferiority, pampering, oversensitivity, and living under too
many aversive experiences. Sexual maladjustment also contributes to the neurotics difficulty. In the final analysis the
neurotic's problems stem from excessive inferiority feelings.

CHAPTER XI

THERAPY

Adlerian therapy rests on the premise that it is an educational (or reeducational) venture involving at least one therapist and one patient. Adler did not set down any strict rules regarding the techniques or progress of therapy. However, he did give us an idea of what the goals of therapy should be (see following).

Usually therapy begins with the complaints of the patient and the situation in which they occur. Then, the patient may tell his or her whole life story, beginning in early childhood. The therapist allows the patient to talk freely and only asks questions when the person stops talking. Fairly early in therapy the doctor will find out where the person fits into the family constellation. Interpretations are not forced on the patient and not given until therapy has progressed far enough that the patient is ready to accept them. Adlerians do not consider the patient cured just when the symptoms have disappeared. The real cure comes only when the patient is able to approach life's problems and assume responsibility for them. Advice is given sparingly. For example, if a person asked the therapist whether she should get a divorce or not, she would probably be told that only she can answer that question. The job of the therapist is to get the patient to recognize the life style. At this point, the patient then will be able to answer the question.

Adler told the story (Orgler, 1963, p. 170) of a woman he met at a party who was to be married for the fourth time. She had divorced the first two husbands and the third had committed suicide. In the fourth, she had found the right man.

Some time later, Adler found out she had just divorced her fifth husband. The point of his story is that some people refuse to recognize themselves for what they are and always put the blame on others for their own faults in life.

Goals of Therapy

With regard to goals of Adlerian therapy Mosak (1979) listed the following:

1. the fostering of social interest,

2. the decrease of inferiority feelings which involve the overcoming of discouragement,

3. a change in the person's style of life which may involve a change in the perception of goals and the transformation of big mistakes into small ones (using the analogy of an automobile, it means a "tune-up" of the engine or a complete "overhaul"),

4. changing faulty motives and faulty values,

5. encouraging the patient to recognize his or her own equality among other people who share the same social community, and/or

6. helping the person to become a contributing member of the group or society (p. 64).

If the patient can reach these objectives, he or she will have feelings of belonging and that he or she is equal to and accepted by other people. The result will be encouragement, optimism, confidence, courage, and security.

Social Interest

One of the basic difficulties of people who have psychological problems such as neuroses, addiction, or delinquency is that they lack social interest. Thus, one of the most pre-eminent goals of therapy is to develop this innate potentiality which Adler identified as social interest (see Ch. IV). Clearly a person who seeks therapy has developed a faulty set of social values. This, in turn, involves a change in his or her style of life. The patient is faced with the choice of maintaining the old ways of behavior which have caused no end of trouble and caused great pain or change and move in some other direction. In the therapeutic process, the patient must learn the mistakes he or she had made which involve the "cheap tricks" and safeguarding devices and find a new and more positive direction in life. Over and over again, Adler stressed the person's free ability to choose. He is able to do or not do as he pleases (Ansbacher & Ansbacher, 1956).

Most all patients who come to therapy lack social interest. They are wound up in themselves and their symptoms. Therefore, one aim of therapy has to be an exercise in cooperation. The therapist must cooperate with the patient in uncovering the mistakes. This is not only for the benefit of the patient but for the welfare of others. Cooperation can only be possible if the patient is of good will and willing to transfer it to the environment. Thus, the patient's first expression of social interest is with the therapist.

Social interest is also kindled by encouragement which comes from many sources in therapy. One learns to have faith in himself or herself and to trust and care. The ultimate goal of therapy is to release the patient's social interest so he or she may become a fellow human being among other human beings. Ideally, in the true Adlerian spirit, the person becomes a true contributor to the betterment of society and one who feels at home in society.

PROGRESS OF THERAPY

In the light of the objectives of therapy, the next matter to be considered is how the therapist is going to accomplish the goals. Mosak (1979) listed the following four methods:

1. **Relationship.** First of all, a good relationship between the patient and the therapist must develop.

2. **Goals.** The therapist must discover the patient's goals and style of life as they affect the ways he or she behaves in contacts with others.

3. **Insight.** What is often called therapeutic insight refers to the patient's ability to discover his or her own errors and what to do to correct them.

4. **Reorientation.** With the insight the final step is a change or a reorientation to a different way of life.

Relationship

In Adlerian therapy, the relationship between the therapist and patient should be friendly and one of equality. Instead of the patient's lying on a couch and free associating as in Freudian therapy, the two sit face to face in chairs that are of the same size. A desk may be avoided since such a piece of furniture involves a distance between the two people and a separation which could impede the therapeutic process.

The general attitude that prevails is that of a creative human being. That is, the patient has created some problems and is responsible for his or her actions. Further, the problems are the fault of faulty learning. Faulty learning can be replaced by appropriate learning and faulty perceptions can be modified. Therapy involves an active cooperation. The goals of both therapist and patient must coincide.

In Freudian therapy, the concept of *transference* is very important, that is, the patient's developing of a strong emotional attachment to the therapist. Adler objected to transference and interpreted it as a condition in which the goals of the therapist and patient were divergent.

Another problem in patient-therapist relationship may be the expectation by the patient of certain reactions from the therapist. Adler referred to these as "scripts" which are similar to what Eric Berne (1964) calls "games." For example, the patient might say, "I'll bet you've never seen a nut like me before," as a challenge to the therapist competence.

The relationship between patient and therapist should promote the educational process. Maybe, for some people, this is their first experience of cooperation and mutual respect. Through therapy, moments of frustration and disagreement are going to occur, but these must be only temporary. Bad relationships don't just happen. They are created by people and the patient must learn that these are the result of wrong interpretation.

Discovering the Life Style and Goals

Analysis begins from the first time the patient enters the therapist's office. Note is made as to how he or she walks, their posture, how they sit. These amount to the discovery of clues in terms of what the patient says and does.

In order to discover the life style, the therapist may begin with the family constellation to discover what was occurring at the time the life style was being established. Here the psychologist or psychiatrist discovers the person's position during early childhood in the family as well as in school and among friends (Shulman & Mosak, 1988).

Next the therapist must probe the patient's earliest recollections (see Ch. VI). Adler felt the earliest memories were excellent indicators of the style of life. These should go back as far as possible. The earliest memories represent the person's fundamental view of life. For example, a woman recalled being picked up by her father only to be placed in a chair so her younger brother could be held. According to Adler, her life style was dominated by persistent fears that others were preferred to her. A man's earliest memory was of falling out of bed. His life style was marked by fear of failure and discouragement.

Another source of information concerning the life style is expressive behavior. The therapist may discover much about the person by observing the overt behavior. Visual expressions, glances, the way the patient walks, and the handshake, all may suggest definite problems. The person with the pampered style of life may like to lean against things, just as he or she used to cling to mother in childhood. Other observations include the patient's movements, the ways patients get up or sit down.

Sometimes the first glance may give an indication of the patient's social attitude.

Like the Freudians and the Jungians, the Adlerians make use of dream analysis as clues to the style of life. Adler said, "Dreams are the factory of emotions." In Chapter VIII, we discussed how dreams could help to discover the style of life.

Besides early recollections, movements, and dreams, other sources open to the therapist include language, all manner of speech and verbal expressions, as well as day dreams. Whether the style of life was good or bad, Adler believed it was consistent so the therapist has available many sources to discover it and by which to assess it.

Therapeutic Insight

Adlerians interpret insight as the understanding of what one's problems are, but also a plan for constructive action. Insight involves an understanding of one's purposes in life. Insight goes further than the "Yes, but . . . " For example, "Yes, I know now what my problems are and what I ought to do about them, but . . . ." Understanding is not enough. Action must follow.

In Adlerian therapy, insight is achieved through the interpretations by the therapist, who takes what he or she can from what is available from the patient in terms of overt behavior, dream fantasies, memories, and symptoms and sees what can be done. In Adler's teleological approach the emphasis is on the future rather than the past. Mosak (1979) suggested the analogy of the mirror being held up to the patient so that he or she can see how they are coping with life. The past is only mentioned to explain to the patient the continuity of the faulty style of life. The therapist may explain the patient's maladaptive behavior in such a way that it appears aversive even by sharing the patient's intentions in such a noxious way that he or she would want to change.

Adlerian therapy makes no use of free association. In some instances, advice is given directly or the therapist may present a number of alternatives from which the patient may choose.

Encouragement is freely given since Adler felt that those people who come for help are in a state of discouragement. An old song which goes, "Accentuate the positive and decentuate the negative . . ." applies to Adlerian therapy. It is always positive. Of course, when mistakes are made they must be corrected. Negative criticism is avoided.

Like many other therapies, Adler's approach avoids being moralistic on the part of the therapist. The patient is not blamed or criticized for his or her problems. The emphasis is not what is *good* or *bad*, but what is *useful* or *useless*. Since many behavior disorders have strong emotional overtones, an appeal to the logical or rational is of little value. On the other hand, cartharsis or confession is encouraged. The idea of "Getting it off your chest" can free the patient from the burdens of holding it in. This is somewhat reminiscent of what Freud picked up from Joseph Breuer in treating Anna O., which became known as the "talking out" cure or "getting it out of your system." Of course, this implies that one has complete trust in the therapist.

Other techniques such as *role playing* or *acting* out may also be helpful.

Reorientation

Eventually, if therapy is successful, a time comes when insight is not enough; but actual behavior must occur. For one to understand what the problems are is fine, but the next step must be, "What am I going to do about them?" Presumably, if the therapist is a good one, he or she has acted as a model for normal behavior. The therapist has a positive style of life and possesses social interest. These qualities of a good therapist will help for behavior change. The therapist will show *warmth* and a *genuine interest* in the patient. The attitude will be one of *encouragement* particularly with regard to changing and improving the patient's behavior. Here, too, the therapist should be a *model* of social interest. The therapist is presented as a good human being without giving the impression of superiority or omnipotence.

The final step following insight must lead to decisive action. Mosak (1979) has suggested a number of techniques which

Adlerian therapists use to promote change. However, he pointed out that they must be used judiciously and appropriately depending on the patient and the situation. Some of these techniques include (1) acting "as if", (2) task setting, (3) creative images, (4) the pushbutton technique, and (5) the "a-ha" experience.

1. **Acting "As If."** In the theater, a seasoned actor has played many roles. This, then, is what the patient might try, that is, playing a different role in life. (Being the good guy instead of the bad guy.) Often the patient will protest indicating that such behavior is "put on" or "phoney". "This 'as if' behavior is not the real me." Thinking about it in a more positive way, one might consider the analogy of putting on a new suit or dress. In former days, women wore hats more frequently. Sometimes when a woman felt down in the dumps, she cheered herself up by going out and buying a new hat or pair of shoes or whatever. Maybe the statement "Clothes make the man" is not absolutely true, but sometimes buying a handsome new suit will make a person feel better. This better feeling may lead to better behavior which is going to be more useful. Sometimes to take on a new role is hard, but if circumstances are right, it can be done.

2. Task Setting. In his book, *Problems of Neuroses* (1929b), Adler suggested to a depressed man that he might go out and do something to make somebody else feel happy. This met with resistance from the person. "How can I do anything to make someone else happy if I can't do anything to make myself happy?" To this Adler replied, "Just think about how you could do it." That would be the first step for thoughts can lead to action. In this instance, we see clearly in Adler the idea of self-determination. One is free to act as he or she chooses and a person can do it if he or she tries hard enough.

Another relative example is what Dunlap (1937) called *negative practice,* or sometimes called the *beta hypothesis.* This involves *practicing* your mistakes, keeping in mind that they *are* mistakes. For the change to occur and the mistakes to be eliminated, the person must be consciously aware of and must have the conscious intent of gettng rid of the error. With regard to problem behavior, one concentrates on his or her symptoms with the intent of getting rid of them.

3. Creating Images. This involves imagining things u. are right, positive, and will work. Imagine that you are at the top of your class or that you worked very hard and won the first prize. These images should be real and not mere "pipe dreams."

4. Pushbutton Technique. Again reference here is to self-determination, that is, a person can create any feeling he or she wishes whether it be pleasant or unpleasant. This means that a person can create whatever feeling he wishes by deciding what he or she wants. We create our own emotions. If we are depressed, it is because we choose to be depressed and likewise happy if we so desire. The situation is as if one had a button in his or her hands and could push it to create whatever emotion was desired.

5. The "A-Ha" Experience. This, of course, is a kind of insight. When one works at a problem for a while he may suddenly "see" the solution. "All of a sudden I understand how it works." This rather sudden understanding into a particular situation or problem comes from greater awareness of oneself as treatment progresses. It involves working at a problem and suddenly finding the solution. When this happens, it generates self-confidence, encouragement, and a willingness to go out and face life's problems in a positive way.

VARIETIES OF ADLERIAN THERAPY

We ordinarily think of Adlerian therapy as a face-to-face situation of two people, patient and therapist. However, other possibilities do exist. One possibility is what Mosak (1979) calls *multiple psychotherapy*. This involves several therapists treating the same patient. This, of course, requires much consultation and meetings among the therapists, but offers certain advantages which involve more than one viewpoint, the introduction of fresh viewpoints, greater objectivity on the part of the therapists and so forth.

Adlerian therapy also can be applied to *groups*. Since most human problems are social, some would suggest that they might better be handled in a group social situation.

Marriage counseling is another variant of Adlerian therapy. In Adler's holistic approach, the couple is treated as a unit. They meet together with the therapist rather than one at a time because they have a joint relationship problem. Here the therapist can observe the joint interaction and engage in a joint effort to the solution of their problems.

Early in Adler's career (see Chapter I), he became involved in establishing child guidance clinics in Vienna. These were helpful for parents, teachers, and children. Today, Adlerian therapy is also applied to *children*. (For a more detailed discussion of Adlerian therapy with children, see Way, 1942, Chapter 9.)

> The focus of therapy (Adlerian) is the encouragement of the individual, the experience of encouragement coming from many avenues in the therapy. The individual learns to have faith in self, to trust and to love. The ultimate, *ideal* goal of psychotherapy is to relase the person's social interest so he may become a fellow human being, a cooperator, a contributor to the creation of a better society, a person who feels belonging and at home in the universe. The person can be said to have actualized himself. Since therapy is learning, theoretically, everyone can change. (Mosak 1979, p. 87)

IMPLICATIONS

Adler never set down any fixed rules as to how the therapist should proceed. Most people seeking therapy have developed faulty styles of life which must be corrected in order to lead productive lives. What follows, then, is that the aim of therapy is reeducation. Other aims of therapy include reduction of feelings of inferiority, the development of social interest, redirecting the style of life, setting up of realistic goals and values, and helping the person to become a contributing member of society.

An important procedure is to assist the person in feeling that he or she belongs and is accepted by other people. Adler stressed "therapeutic insight" on the part of the patient which involves an understanding of what one's problems are and a plan for constructive action. This insight is gained through the help of the therapist who interprets the person's symptoms, early memories, and dreams. Finally, once the person understands what the problems are, he or she must do something about them.

When therapy is successful, the individual learns to have faith in himself or herself so one can be a useful human being, one who can cooperate and contribute to the betterment of society.

CRIME AND ITS PREVENTION

Unlike other of the psychodynamic theorists such as Freud, Jung, and the Neo-Freudians (Horney, Fromm, and Sullivan), Adler was concerned with the problems of crime and delinquency, as well as their prevention and treatment. We noted in Chapter VII that one of the three main problems in life has to do with choosing and pursuing a vocation. In our jobs we, in some way, contribute to the welfare of others. The vast majority of criminals are untrained and lack the skills necessary for some kind of useful work. This goes back to early life where the child showed a lack of interest in working.

We find the same kind of failure in criminals as we do in problem children, neurotics, psychotics, alcoholics, and sexual perverts. They all fail in their approach to the problems of life. All lack social interest showing little concern for the welfare of their fellow human beings.

All people strive for superiority, from defeat to victory or from below to above. In all criminal actions and attitudes, clearly criminals are striving to overcome difficulties. Some criminals come from good backgrounds and others from poor ones. The basic difference between the criminal and the normal person is that the goal of criminals does not include any usefulness to society. In order to understand the criminal we must take to account the nature of his or her failure in cooperation.

Adler felt that the economic situation of the criminal was *not* the basic reason for criminal behavior, but rather the answer is to be found in a faulty style of life, an inability to face life's problems. Criminals are not interested in others. Their ability to cooperate is limited and that limit is exhausted when they turn to crime.

Adler felt the criminal has three problems. The first is one of relationship with others. The criminal may have friends, but they are only of his or her own kind. They form gangs or mobs and show only loyalty to one another. They cannot make friends with society at large. The second problem lies with their occupation. They will say to you, "You don't know the terrible conditions of labor" (Adler, 1931, p. 202). A useful occupation involves an interest in other people. The criminal grows up unprepared to meet the problems of work. The majority of them are unskilled and untrained. In a similar manner, they are untrained in cooperation, even when they were in school. The third problem involves care and love. They consider their sex partners as a piece of property. Their molls and prostitutes belong to them, and will be paid for in some way or another, whether it be money or some other personal advantage.

Criminals look, speak, and listen in a different way from normal people. When a normal person speaks, the intention is that others will understand what they are saying. The criminal has a private logic and a private intelligence. A criminal will say, "I saw a man with nice trousers and I didn't, so I had to kill him" (Adler, 1931, p. 204). The criminal has no need to make a useful living. That would be too much work.

Basically, all criminals are cowards. They avoid the problems of living which they cannot handle. They guard themselves in their crimes by darkness and with their weapons. Crime is a coward's imitation of heroism. In their cowardice they are evading the problems they are not strong enough to solve. As cowards, they think they are heroes and enhance their vanity by overcoming the police or by not being discovered in their crimes. Like neurotics, they suffer from an inferiority complex. Actually, the criminal feels incapable of normal success. In many cases, he or she will hide their inferiority by developing a "cheap" superiority complex. They act tough and strong. They boss people around when, in reality, they are frightened.

In the criminal, the striving is for a personal superiority, which is unusually fictitious.

DEVELOPMENT OF THE CRIMINAL PERSONALITY

Almost always, the problems of the criminal began in early family experience. As a child, the developing criminal had problems as all children do; but no one around was able to help in the solutions. Many criminals come from families with bad reputations, but not always. Some come from so-called "good" families. In Adler's view, unlike many sociologists, the environment alone will not breed criminals. For whatever reason, perhaps spoiling or neglect, the potential criminal fails to develop social interest. Adler felt that the criminal style of life had already developed by the age of four or five. From then on, the child deceives himself or herself with the feeling that he or she is neglected. These children feel deprived and unloved. Even as children, they may steal as a compensation for their feelings of being unwanted. When old enough for school, these children will often play truant. In avoiding going to school, they often find others who share the same experiences and have taken the same route. The other truants engage in flattery and give hope for becoming a useless member of society. According to Adler, this is the way that thousands of children form criminal gangs in which they see the world as their enemy; and only fellow criminals become their friends.

A child's first social contact is with the mother. Perhaps, she was not skillful enough to draw the child into cooperation. During the school years, he or she has difficulty in making friends with other children. They hate school, schoolwork, their school mates, and their teachers. Likewise, the possibility of organ inferiority may lead to strong generalized feelings of inferiority. For many reasons, the child becomes hostile to the school situation. The entire world of normal people becomes their enemy. Only their fellow "criminals" become their friends.

PREVENTION

Since the first contact of cooperation and social interest lies with the mother (or in today's working world, the father may be the one who has the major contact in early years with the child), she must understand how to enlarge the bonds of cooperation and social interest. She must behave in such a way that the child will be concerned with other people outside the family. If the mother keeps the child all to herself, a pampered style of life will result. A failure of social concern can be the starting point of a criminal career.

REHABILITATION

If we are to alter the criminal behavior, we must find the roots of the difficulty. In order to discover why criminals are failures, one must first find out the circumstances which provoke their failures. We must find out where the failures first began and the circumstances which surrounded them.

Adler felt strongly that capital punishment was not the solution to rehabilitating the criminals. This only reinforces the attitude that society is against them. With the use of capital punishment, the police become the targets of their defiance. The basic solution is to find the block which has interfered with cooperation, which was first experienced in childhood. Ordinarily, most criminals have some degree of cooperation, except for the demands of social living. Furthermore, the criminal has chosen the wrong means of overcoming inferiority and fulfilling the basic drive for superiority. The therapist, counselor, or social worker must show the criminal where he or she has chosen the wrong means and why. A person must be trained in courage, to be interested in others and to cooperate with them. If the criminal understands that crime is really cowardice and not courage, the greatest impetus to crime will be removed and, if all of society understands this, then no child will be trained for a life of crime. The key is to be found in a mistaken style of life. All cooperation has to be learned, but the potentiality for cooperation and social interest is in everyone. The possibility of social interest in inherent in everyone.

In discussing the order of birth (see pp. 64-67), Adler has suggested that the first born, who later becomes "dethroned," thwarted, and put in the back seat, is more prone to develop a criminal career. The first born can feel deprived and, as an unhealthy compensation, begin to steal. Of course, this is far from inevitable. Any child in the family constellation can become a potential criminal. Perhaps other siblings are preferred and favored. A prudent mother and father will take care not to show favoritism to one and neglect the other children.

Adler suggested that sometimes one of the other children might happen to be extremely intelligent and gifted. It is easy to favor such a child while the others suffer. Sometimes the parents are constantly complaining of bad times and poor circumstances in the presence of their children. This kind of action can set up a block to social interest. The same thing can happen if the parents are always criticizing others, their relatives, and neighbors, expressing bad feelings and prejudice. Such attitudes will lead the children into a distasteful view of what their fellow men and women are like. When social interest is blocked, only an egotistical attitude is left. The child says, "Why should I do anything for other people?" (Adler, 1931, p. 222). Such favoritism, pampering, and criticism should all be avoided. If parents are fair and show social interest, teaching cooperation, many problems can be avoided. Children with organ inferiorities can be led to develop appropriate compensations, but it must be nurtured. Adler emphasized the fact that a person well-trained in cooperation and social interest will not become a criminal, but if this is not recognized, we cannot hope to avoid the unhappy consequences of crime.

CHARACTERISTICS SUMMARIZED

In his book, *What Life Should Mean To You*, (1931), Adler summarized what he considers to be the main points in his scientific investigation of crime as follows:

1. Criminals are born no different from other people. No basic tendency to crime is inherited as some psychologists would suggest.

2. The criminal has trained himself or herself in non-cooperative ways of thinking and acting.

3. Very early in life, during the first four or five years, a block has occurred in the development of social interest. This block has been set up in the family situation and in the treatment of the child by the parents and others close to the child.

4. The criminal differs from other failures in life in that he or she has lost the desire to achieve success (superiority) in the normal tasks of life.

5. The activity level of the criminal has been directed to the useless side of life. Here, the criminal differs from other failures on one point in particular. That is, he or she tends to have a high activity level (see Chapter VI). In this way, he or she differs from the neurotic or alcoholic, who typically have low activity levels. In this activity, he or she takes from others for whatever they want which is not given voluntarily.

6. Criminal activity arises when a person is in a difficulty but lacks the courage to face it in a cooperative way. The criminal looks for the easy solution.

7. In all of the preceding, we can observe an inferiority complex. The criminal is running away from the tasks of life. He or she may mask the inferiority by developing a "cheap" superiority complex.

8. The roots of criminal behavior are to be found in a style of life which can involve organ inferiority, pampering or neglect.

REMEDIES

Adler also offers some remedies.

1. The development of greater occupational training and skills. The criminal so frequently turns to crime because he or she does not know how to work at a useful job.

2. We should avoid in our social life all things that act as a challenge to the criminal. These include great extremes of poverty and luxury.

3. We should not delude ourselves in the belief that criminals are going to be terrified by the thought of capital punishment. The thought of this punishment only adds to the excitement of the criminal game. The thrill is in committing a crime and not being caught.

4. The best solution to the inhibition of crime is to train children in cooperation and social interest. Such children will not be inclined or allured into crime.

Adler did not suggest that all those who commit crimes should be allowed to do so. Laws are made for the protection of society. Criminals may have to be apprehended in order to protect society. One solution is the development of probation officers who can check on the released criminal so that such crimes are not repeated. We need a police force to protect society from criminals. His main point is that, capital punishment, electrocution, or hanging are not the solutions in the long run and will not deter crime on the part of others.

IMPLICATIONS

The basic problem with criminals is that they never learned a useful occupation.

They have failed in their approach to life and lack social interest.

They never learned to cooperate with others.

Criminals are cowards. They are afraid to face up to the problems of everyday living. To be useful citizens requires too much effort. They see crime as the easy way out.

To prevent crime, occupational training should begin early in life. This early training includes learning to cooperate and being interested in others.

Capital punishment is not the solution in eliminating crime. The thought of it on the part of the criminal only adds to the thrill of the crime. Executions by hanging or electrocution are inadequate solutions of the elimination of criminal behavior.

Reeducation and rehabilitation are the best solutions for the elimination of future crimes.

APPLICATIONS TO EDUCATION

Adler believed that for the development of normal human personalities an extremely important aspect was to correctly bring up the person from the very beginning. In order to rear a child properly, one must first understand the child. If adults are difficult to understand, children are even more so. Too often we look at the child from the eyes of an adult and impose on him or her the things we expect but are not there. Many people view children as they would desire them to be and not as they really are. If we are to follow the guidelines of Individual Psychology, our task is to lead the child in developing those abilities necessary for a favorable character development. Since the style of life is developed during the first four or five years, the upbringing during these years is of crucial importance.

MOTHER

Adler presumed that since most fathers work and spend less time with the child, the mother is most responsible for the child's rearing. She will be the primary influence in the child's development. The suggestion has been made that Adler overemphasized the role of the mother. Whether or not this is so is an arguable issue. His observations were that geniuses were strongly influenced by their mothers even though the mothers were neither artistic nor intellectual. The ideal mother (or teacher, for that matter) is *understanding, benevolent, cheerful, reliable, patient,* and above all *optimistic.*

Proper education involves setting the right goals for the child. From the very beginning the child must gradually be prepared to tackle life's problems. In many cases, complaints arising out of organ inferiority may be cured by a physician. In cases where the organ inferiority cannot be corrected, the child must be led to develop appropriate compensations.

In the upbringing of a child, Adler stressed, in particular, *tenderness*. He said if we are in love, we must be tender. As mentioned many times, Adler warned against pampering or spoiling. *Spoiling* involves depriving a child of independence, not giving the child a chance to accomplish something for himself or herself, thus preventing the child from using his or her own initiatives. Through *pampering* the child is brought up to be a parasite on society. Pampering should not be confused with tenderness. One can be tender and still allow the youngster to be independent. One can spoil a child, and not be tender, by forcing the child to be dependent on the adult.

Adler regarded the Oedipus complex to be the result of a pampered upbringing. The so-called hatred for the father in the Oedipus complex is nothing more than a striving for power by a spoiled child who does not care to endure the father's authority.

Likewise, *neglect* will have unfortunate consequences. Orgler recalls a story which Adler told her (Orgler, 1963, p. 134): A woman exclaimed to Adler in her son's presence, "I never wanted this child." One can easily enough understand why the child developed hostile feelings. Not uncommonly a child will feel neglected when, in actuality, he or she is not. The fault lies in the child's attitude and, in these cases, the mother must change the child's views.

Nagging, reproaching, and threatening are, for many parents, a common means of bringing up the child. This kind of behavior should be avoided, because it will only lead to an increase in the child's feelings of inferiority. Some children will react to nagging by being stubborn. They will throw their heads back, clench their fists, and become negativistic.

PUNISHMENT

All children are going to make mistakes and be naughty at times. In Adler's view, scolding is the wrong technique for correcting behavior. For example, a better procedure is to draw the child's attention to mistakes indirectly. Instead of helping the child, scolding only leads to discouragement. Praise when a child does better and encouragement for improvement will be far more fruitful. Adler opposed corporal punishment by spanking, beating, or whipping. These techniques only enhance a child's feeling of inferiority. Particularly, the young child does not understand why he or she was so punished. Older children will only become more hostile. In many cases, harsh punishment leads to fear which is not the proper motivation for the child. Recent research has indicated that abused children grow up to become abusing parents. Adler was acutely aware of this from his own observations when he reported a child who said following a whipping, "When I am grown up, then I will marry and then I shall be Daddy and I'll do the beating" (Orgler, 1963, p. 156). B.F. Skinner, the prominent behaviorist, has opposed punishment when he demonstrated through his own experimental research (1938) the uselessness of punishment. Those who favor punishment of children claim that it will eliminate the bad behavior immediately. The change in behavior may be immediately apparent; but, in Skinner's research, punishment only suppresses behavior temporarily and does not eliminate it. Both Adler and Skinner pointed out that the ultimate consequences of punishment are negative. Adler pointed out that one must consider the feelings of the child. Punishment only fosters hatred and resentment. In the long run, a pattern of beating or whipping leads to a faulty style of life in which the child grows up to adulthood by becoming hard and cold, lacking in social interest.

Parents should be acutely aware that they want their children to grow up with social feeling. If the father becomes the source of punishment and the mother says to the child, "If you don't behave, I'll tell your father," or "Just wait until your father gets home and you will get your spanking," all of this only instills anxiety and hatred for the father. Interestingly many years later, B.F. Skinner (1953) demonstrated experimentally that the anticipation of inevitable punishment becomes the paradigm for anxiety.

FAMILY

Children need to grow up with the attitude that their parents are fellow human beings. The harmony between the parents leaves a lasting impression on the child. If the parents quarrel and criticize other people in the presence of the child, then the child learns to regard the world as hostile. In a peaceful, benevolent, and cheerful home atmosphere, the child will view the world as a good place to be. In particular, Adler stressed the importance of harmony at the dinner table (or breakfast table) when all the family has gathered together.

Parents must make sure that they do not instigate rivalry between the children. This is particularly important in the family constellation. Since the first born often becomes the "dethroned king" when the second child comes along, the parents must take special steps to prepare the first born for the arrival of the second. The first born may be told that he or she is going to have a new playmate. Later on the first born can be called upon to assist in little tasks, for example, when the new baby is having a bath or being fed. These techniques will instill an interest in others on the part on the first born.

Sometimes parents will hold up one child as an example to the others. This is intended to spur the others on, but this approach is more likely to lead to a resentment toward the example and destroy the harmony between the children. A happy solution is to encourage interests in different fields for each child, so no one will feel restricted in a particular field of interest by another brother or sister. Each child will be able to develop freely without fear of competition from the others.

As the child grows older, he or she will engage in play and sports activities with other children. This can help foster a child's interest in others. In these activities children learn to cooperate with each other. Children who do not learn cooperation will grow up to be supreme egotists who operate only for their own advantage.

In order to prepare a child for a vocation, the child must learn to experience pleasure from his or her own achievements. A good procedure is to put little obstacles in the way which a child can overcome. Then the achievement may be praised (not the child). This will encourage the child to try further tasks. Some people think praise is a bad thing, that it will lead to conceit. However, Adler believed that most children understand the merit of their achievements and know when praise is justified.

SCHOOL

After the family, the school is the next most important for the development of social living. Adler said, "School is the prolonged arm of the family. It would be our hope if all the teachers could be well trained, that psychologists would become unnecessary" (Adler, 1931, p. 156).

A truly competent teacher will understand the child's difficulties and take appropriate corrective measures. A good educator will train the child in cooperation. Adler favored cooeducation to the education of the sexes separately, thus allowing greater cooperation between the sexes. He believed that special classes for the "slow" learners are questionable because they are more likely to produce intense inferiority feelings among their members. Like the therapist, teachers must be well adjusted, and experienced in social living so they can act as models for the children.

A common premise among some school teachers is that bad marks will spur children on. This is bad psychology. Too often bad marks lead to discouragement, and the children will quit trying. The substitution is encouragement. Often a lack of abilty has its real source in a lack of interest in a task. Sometimes this lack is really a lack of self confidence. Also, a poor performance could be the result of impoverished circumstances, never prepared at home, a lack of intellectual training, or too much work to be done at home. All of these problems could prevent the child from obtaining the same success at school as the more fortunate children. An understanding teacher is needed to help such children.

SEX

Children also must be prepared for love problems later in life. A child should never be in doubt as to whether the child is a boy or a girl. Girls should learn that becoming a mother is not an inferior role. Both boys and girls should learn that, although they are different, they are equal. Children should not sleep in the same room with the parents, nor observe intercourse between the parents. When a child asks a question about sex, the answer should be limited to the question and explained at a level that he or she can understand. Sexuality should neither be overvalued nor undervalued.

ADOLESCENCE

Puberty and adolescence bring their own problems. This is a period of transition filled with uncertainty and doubt. During this period, some industrious children suddenly become lazy, or some children judged previously dull suddenly become brilliant. The parent or teacher must realize that they no longer have a child before them. Adolescents must be allowed more freedom as they grow up. Sometimes parents try to keep the youngest child from growing up. He is referred to still as "little Joe" or she is called "little Mary". Parents must realize that children must be allowed to grow up.

On the other hand, some adolescents resort to more childish behavior, because they fear the changes which take place during puberty. Since girls mature about two years earlier than do boys, the boys can easily develop inferiority feelings because they are so "little" and want to be "big." The masculine protest of the girl appears clearly during adolescence. She may defy her parents by taking on a lover just to annoy them. Here Adler strongly advised avoiding events which typically lead to protests on the part of the adolescent. Furthermore, he strongly advised parents against taking on an authoritarian attitude towards the youngsters. If the adolescent appears defiant, this did not suddenly just happen. The attitude existed before puberty began. Adler advised against trying to alter the specific defiant behavior since the problem went much deeper. The adolescent's whole attitude must be changed. Adler did not believe that defiance was an inevitable part of adolescence. From early childhood, parents should not play the authoritarian role.

During adolescence, some young people are led astray and get into trouble. Adler's advice on prevention was to be sure that in childhood the individual was developing a positive life style. The child must learn to think independently and to assume responsibility. This kind of training will assure that the person will be able to resist bad influences.

The kind of education that Individual Psychology prescribes is to understand the child thoroughly and to avoid any disturbance in the developing of his or her character by authoritarian means. The child must be led down the right path without force. The education has fulfilled its task when the child evidences adaptability, optimism, self-confidence, courage, social interest, and cooperation and shows a concern for contributing to the welfare of others.

IMPLICATIONS

The early education of the child begins with the mother. Proper education involves setting the right goals early in life. The attitudes of the mother should be understanding and benevolent. The mother should be cheerful, reliable, optimistic, and tender. Praise and encouragement are far more effective than punishment. However, the mother should praise and encourage the child's proper **behavior,** not the child alone.

Next to the mother, the family is the second most important agency in the education of the child. The home atmosphere should be peaceful and caring. Another brother or sister or another friend of the child should never be held up as an example. This will only foster the resentment.

After the family, the school plays a decisive role in the proper education of the child. A competent teacher who understands the child's difficulties will take appropriate measures to correct their pupil's failings. A good teacher will train pupils in cooperation. Rather than give bad marks to encourage the child to do better, a good teacher will use positive means in encouraging the child to succeed.

CHAPTER **XIV**

ADLER'S CRITIQUE
OF FREUDIAN THEORY

In 1902, Freud invited Adler and a number of other Viennese physicians to meet for discussions of his theories. This was the beginning of the Vienna Psychoanalytic Society. Adler never considered himself a Freudian, nor was he ever psychoanalyzed. However, he had defended Freud's *Interpretation of Dreams* (1900), which had been lambasted by the press. In those days, Adler became a co-editor, along with Freud and William Stekel of Freud's journal, *Zeutralblatt fur Psychoanalyse.* Many biographers (Jones, 1955; Orgler 1963; Ansbacher & Ansbacher, 1956) agree that Freud and Adler were never close friends. As time passed, their theoretical differences became acute. In 1911, Adler was asked to present three papers before the Vienna Psychoanalytic Society in which he pointed out the differences between Freud's and his own theories. The differences were so great that Adler resigned from the society and his editorship of the journal, thus ending any further contacts between himself and Freud. Adler and a few of his followers in the Society started the Society for Free Psychoanalysis, which later became the Society for Individual Psychology.

UNCONSCIOUS

Even before Freud set forth his theory of the unconscious, the idea of an unconscious mind was not new. Leibnitz, in the seventeenth century, had suggested degrees of consciousness (or unconsciousness) and Herbart later set forth the idea of a conflict between ideas in consciousness and unconsciousness. Freud introduced, along with Joseph Breuer, the idea of free association whereby ideas in the unconscious could be purged and brought into consciousness. Likewise, dream analysis was useful in getting at the unconscious, because dreams arose from desires in the unconscious. According to Freud, a certain dream censorship always exists on the part of consciousness as to what aspects of the wishes may be allowed out. During sleep, the censor is partially relaxed, and certain painful unconscious elements may get by the censorship by taking disguised forms. These disguises could take the form of dream symbols. First of all, Adler objected to the dichotomy between consciousness and unconsciousness as a kind of old-fashioned dualism in the division of the mind into two parts. For Adler, the entire personality was a unity not to be split into parts. Furthermore, in all aspects of his theory, Freud was a complete determinist. Things had causes and often the causes were to be found in the unconscious. Adler stressed the idea of teleology: how future goals can affect present behavior. Thus, Adler opposed an idea of a "dynamic unconscious" which brings with it the conception of strong forces residing in the unconscious. Rather than making a distinction between consciousness and unconsciousness, Adler believed one must think of things as a whole. Adler did not deny the unconscious completely. For him, it amounted to memories, motives, feelings and attitudes which might be thought to exist at the periphery of consciousness.

LIBIDO THEORY

In Freud's early writings, the libido was an energy force which was basically sexual in nature, so the sex drive became the ultimate source of our psychic energy. For Freud, dreams were wish fulfilling and, in most cases, dream symbols represented intercourse or various aspects of the sexual apparatus (enclosures: houses, boxes = the female genitalia; long, pointed objects: pencils, church steeples, pens = the penis. Fruit: peaches, pears, apples = women's breasts; riding a horse, going up and down stairs = intercourse and so forth). Libido was the name for the sex energy. Later, of course, Freud modified his theory of dynamic forces into a division between the life and death instincts. Life instincts included hunger, thirst, sex which existed in opposition to the death instinct or desire to destroy, which eventually wins out.

In any event, Adler believed Freud had completely over-valued the sex instinct. Adler's dynamic striving was more general and was expressed in a number of ways, as the striving from below to above, or a striving for superiority or perfection. Adler considered Freud's pan-sexualism (sex is everywhere) as a misrepresentation of the facts.

SOCIETY

For Freud, the existence of a society was merely a derivitive of the sex instinct. Sexual repression was what drove people to unite. Freud felt a certain antithesis between sex and society. In highly developed societies, sex was displaced or sublimated into higher cultural values: art, music, literature; and, conversely, when society became degenerative or archaic, sex became promiscuous and unregulated.

For Freud, another function involved the role of women in society. Woman's place was in the home. Her duties involved taking care of the household, begetting and caring for children. In the household duties is where she could make up for the lack of a penis. Adler favored the complete equality of the sexes.

Adler is considered to be the first of the social analysts. He stressed as an inherent potentiality the need for social interest. Man is inherently a social animal and the well-adjusted person directs his or her strivings for superiority in the direction of an improvement of society and human welfare. Society was not derived from sexual repression but arose out of our inherently social tendencies. In Freudian theory, the concept of social interest is lacking. He felt man is basically narcissistic and driven by the pleasure principle. As far as the molding of the personality, Freud did not appeal to the forces of the group or culture as did Adler.

If any implication of social interest is in Freudian theory, it will be found merely as a means of furthering the demands of adaptation. Freud was strongly influenced by Darwinian theory. Society exists merely as a deterrent to chaos. Without society, a war of all would exist against all, but culture contradicts the pleasure principle.

RELIGION

Freud's attack on religion is expressed in the fact that it tends to thwart the sex instinct. Instead of being the primary driving force, Adler considered sex to be a refreshment to life which reaffirms personal values and a kinship with the human race.

Freud considered religious beliefs to be extremely dangerous and harmful both to the individual and to the society. Religion was viewed as a regression to infancy where a person is helpless to deal with the threats of the environment and looks for the protection of an all powerful God. Religion becomes an illusion whereby one tries to master the real world and engages in the fantasy of wish fulfillment. Religion is a deterrent to reason and intelligence. Most of us are indoctrinated with religion as children before we are able to apply reason. We become caught up in its effect like a narcotic. In *The Future of an Illusion* (1956), Freud has written some of the strongest attacks on religion ever published.

Adler was born into the Jewish faith, but became converted to Christianity. His views on religion are not as positive as those presented by Jung. Adler's consideration of religion is more lukewarm. The Christian precepts of "Love thy neighbor" and "It is more blessed to give than to receive" are desirable expressions of social interest. He regarded Freud's rejection of these dictates as the selfish expression of a pampered child. The function of religion is to increase social interest and enhance social living. God can become the model of self perfection. Also, religion can help restore a faulty style of life.

REPRESSION

Adler objected to Freud's analogy of comparing his system to the sciences of physics and chemistry. In using the concepts borrowed from these sciences (force, energy, etc.), Freud had hoped that his psychology could eventually be reduced to physiology and chemistry. Freud's concept of repression involved the ego's use of its psychic energy to take conscious, unpleasant experiences, and shove them into the unconscious; and the ego's use of its own psychic energy to hold in check those unpleasant memories now existing in the unconscious. The taking of conscious, painful experiences and forcing them into the unconscious Freud ordinarly identified as *repression proper.* The possibility always existed that the ego could engage its psychic energy to keep in the unconscious those threatening impulses with which we were born and block them so they never reach consciousness. This, Freud identified as *primal repression.*

Adler considered the whole idea of repression as a matter of circular reasoning. Accordingly, he wrote: "Repression takes place under the pressure of culture, under the pressure of ego drives. In giving this explanation, the thoughts of an abnormal sexual constitution, of sexual prematurity are resorted to: Question: Where does our culture come from? Answer: From the repression" (Adler, 1956, p. 61). This becomes a kind of "the chicken and the egg" problem. Which came first?

Instead of repression, Adler preferred to substitute his safeguarding tendencies (see Chapter IX). Futhermore, repression assumes the existence of an unconscious mind which becomes the receptable of the repressed ideas. Since Adler did not make any clear distinction between consciousness and unconsciousness, the existence of such a reservoir for repressed ideas or memories appears fictitious.

OEDIPUS COMPLEX

The Oedipus complex is one of the corner stones of Freudian theory. For Freud, such a complex is universal in all of us, men and women. At about the age of five, the complex emerges from deep in the unconscious, but never completely reaches consciousness. However, it has many outward manifestations. In the boy, it becomes an intensification of his sexual attraction to the mother and fear and antagonism for the father. In the girl, it develops a strong, sexual attachment for the father and a hostility toward the mother because she brought her daughter into the world devoid of a penis (penis envy).

For Adler, the matter is quite simple. First of all, he sees no evidence of the universality of the Oedipus complex. Secondly, when it does exist, it is merely the result of excessive pampering. The Oedipus complex is in no way a fundamental fact of life, but becomes a vicious, unnatural result of maternal (or paternal) overindulgence.

According to Adler, "This comes more clearly into view when the boy or the youth in his inordinate vanity sees himself betrayed by girls and has not developed sufficient social interest to be able to mix with other people" (Adler, 1938, p. 22).

MASCULINE PROTEST

In Adler's later interpretation of the masculine protest, it was a protest on the part of women against their subservient positon in society. He considered the sexes to be equal and that they should be treated as such. In our society, history records the emancipation of women. As pointed out earlier in this chapter, Freud believed woman's place was in the home. Her duties were keeping house and caring for the children. If any counterpart exists to the masculine protest in Freudian theory, it would be found in the concept of penis envy, whereby the girl resents her mother because she bore her and brought her into the world without a penis.

OTHER DIFFERENCES

From these comparisons between Freud and Adler, one can understand why their association lasted only ten years. Even before their final break, a cooling off had occurred in their relationship. Other differences also existed. Freud was basically pessimistic about people. In the end, the death wish wins out. On the other hand, Adler was basically optimistic about people. We are all born with the potentiality of social interest and hence have the capacity for the improvement of ourselves along with the betterment of society.

Freud was a thorough-going determinist. Adler stressed the future goals towards which we all strive. In therapy, Freud stressed free association, the talking-out method. Adler felt such a technique was too time consuming. Through free association, Freud believed the unconscious must be flushed out, repression must be lifted so the ego may use it's store of psychic energy for better purposes in achieving the pleasure princple rather than being used up in suppressing unpleasant ideas. For Adler, therapy was directed towards developing a better style of life, substituting a more positive outlook for the faulty style of life, and developing of social interest.

IMPLICATIONS

1. Adler stressed the human personality as a unitary whole in contrast to Freud's division into the (a) ego, (b) super ego, and (c) id and a division between the unconscious and the conscious.

2. Adler proposed an upward striving force which he identified as striving for superiority or self enhancement in contrast to Freud's division between the life and death instincts with an over emphasis on the sex drive.

3. Adler believed in man's inherent potentiality for social interest, a striving for the betterment of society in contrast to Freud's structuring of society merely to avoid the chaos of the opposing instincts of life and death.

4. Adler stressed an equality of the sexes and the emancipation of women to achieve sexual equality as opposed to Freud's belief in the subservient role of women whose purpose was to bear and raise children and care for the home.

5. Adler believed that religion could be useful through its fostering of social intererst (Love thy neighbor as thy self). Freud viewed religion as a regression to infantile help-

lessness, an illusion, a fantasy of wish fulfillment (the protective, almighty God).

6. In Adler's conception, the Oedipus Complex may be the result of excessive pampering in contrast to Freud's belief in its inborn universality.

7. Adler was basically optimistic toward human nature while Freud was basically pessimistic. In the end the death instinct eventually wins out.

8. Adler stressed the value of therapy as a means of restructuring a faulty style of life and fostering social interest while Freud's aim for therapy was the flushing out of unconscious sources of troubles through free association.

CHAPTER

EPILOGUE

Adlerian psychology gained recognition in the United States during the 1930s and 1940s, particularly when Adler and some of his students, in particular, Rudolph Dreikurs, settled in America. Dreikurs (1950) continued to propagate Individual Psychology until his death in 1972. Other leading proponents of Adler's psychology have been Ansbacher and Ansbacher (1956) and Mosak (1973, 1979).

Among recent personality theorists, Adler has strongly influenced Abraham Maslow and Carl Rogers, leading humanistic psychologists on the contemporary scene. Above all, like them, Adler was a humanist. He cared for people and their welfare. Leading existential psychologists such as Victor Frankl and Rollo May, along with Adler, have been concerned with the meaning of life.

SUMMARY OF ADLER'S POSITION

To become a part of society is a universal aspect of all human beings. The desire for the betterment of other people was identified by Adler as *social interest*. This tendency or potentiality is in all of us, but it must be developed. If it is not nurtured in the family constellation, likely children will develop more useless activities. The kinds of behavior that *works* by involving a person with other people is the behavior that gets established in any individual personality. After Adler died, his colleague and follower, Rudolph Dreikurs, actually used the term, "reinforcer" (Pratt, 1985). The interpretation of this term, which means to strengthen behavior, seems compatible with modern learning theory (Skinner, 1971). Furthermore, Adler used the term "environment" in much the same way as contemporary psychologists do. Social interest means a feeling of belonging to all of humanity and through it cooperation and a division of labor can occur. Such a division is a pre-requisite for the development of any civilized society. Conceit, self-centeredness and pathological behavior arise out of a lack of social interest. Most all of the misfits in a society lack social interest.

Each of us selects our own life goals and styles of life by making use of a variety of ways of achieving them. Adler stressed future strivings rather than causality in the molding of the human personality. We create our own life style by the age of four or five. This can be discovered in a number of ways: by recalling earliest memories, the analysis of dreams and general observation of a person's activities. A faulty style of life inevitably originates in childhood resulting in abnormal behavior through pampering, neglect, or inappropriate compensations for organ inferiorities.

The primary motivating force in all of us is the striving for superiority (or self-perfection). These strivings arise, in part, out of the child's feelings of inferiority. These feelings are normal in all of us and relate closely to how the child perceives the world, perhaps, as an overwhelming environment. The strivings for superiority in a normal person will be guided by his or her social interest or lack of it. In psychologically disturbed persons, such as neurotics, addicts or criminals, the strivings are guided by selfish desires where a lack of social interest prevails. In healthy personalities, the feelings of inferiority will give rise to appropriate compensations. So compensation is going to be a normal part of living. When the child is exposed to the wrong environment, he or she may be overwhelmed by helplessness. This, in turn, will lead to the inferiority complex which is the starting point for abnormal behavior. In some instances, the wrong compensation leads to the superiority complex which expresses itself in authoritarian ways, and even tyranny.

Adler's approach to the human personality was holistic. He considered a human being as a dynamic unity which always operates as a whole. Unlike Freud, Adler did not divide personality into parts. He disdained a distinction between consciousness and unconsciousness.

Adler applied his psychology in many areas: psychotherapy, education, and the study and prevention of criminal behavior. The goal of therapy was to create a better style of life which involved social interest and an orientation toward other people, along with a concern for human welfare. Education begins with the mother and her ways of bringing up the child. The child should be loved but not pampered. He or she must be taught cooperation and sharing. Later on, the school takes over in fostering further cooperation and an interaction between the sexes. Criminals are made, not born. Their wayward ways begin in childhood where they do not learn the importance of work and the division of labor.

ADLER'S PSYCHOLOGY, PRO AND CON

Individual Psychology has had its adherents as well as its critics. It has been criticized (1) for offering an oversimplified interpretation of personality. Adler did not use complicated constructs. He was a practical man and never intended to be a profound scholar. Critics have also suggested that (2) he overemphasized feelings of inferiority (just as Freud was criticized for overemphasizing sex), and (3) the importance of social factors in the molding of personalities. (4) His methodology was observational rather than experimental. Others have maintained that (5) he was unrealistic concerning the nature of people. He was overly optimistic in a world where hatred abounds. Those who prefer objectivity claim (6) that Adler was too subjective. They complain that such concepts as the creative self (creative power) and fictional final goals are illusory and ill-defined. These concepts cannot be put to any empirical test. Of course, the same criticism also can be levied against Freud and Jung (Freud's libido, psychic energy, cathexis and Jung's collective unconscious).

On the positive side, in the light of contemporary psychology, Adler can be credited with stressing the importance of social factors in personality development. He championed the equality of the sexes, the importance of the family in a child's rearing and the importance of having goals in life towards which we all strive. His psychology is pragmatic, useful and easy to understand. Finally, Individual Psychology can get high marks when it comes to applications: to abnormal psychology, psychotherapy, work, education, and the study of crime and its prevention. Even though Adler died in 1937, institutes for the study and advancement of Individual Psychology are very prominent today throughout the western world. His psychology is not a "dead" system, merely to be studied by scholars merely interested in the past. The concept of the masculine protest abounds today in a society where the sexes are now becoming recognized as equal. Most educated persons have heard of compensations and the feelings of inferiority.

BIBLIOGRAPHY

Adler, A. (Alexandria) (1941). The psychology of repeated accidents in industry. *American Journal of Psychiatry*, Vol. 98, pp. 99-102.

Adler, A. (Alfred) (1917). *A study of organ inferiority and its psychical compensations.* New York: Nervous and Mental Disease Publishing.

Adler, A. (1921). *The neurotic consitution.* London: Kegan Paul.

Adler, A. (1925). *Practice and theory of individual psychology.* London: Routledge and Kegan Paul.

Adler, A. (1926). *The neurotic constitution.* New York: Dodd, Mead.

Adler, A. (1927). *Understanding human nature.* Grenwich, CT: Fowcett.

Adler, A. (1929a). *The science of living.* New York: Greenberg Publishers.

Adler, A. (1929b). *The problem of neuroses.* London: Kegan Paul.

Adler, A. (1931). *What life should mean to you.* Boston: Little, Brown.

Adler, A. (1933). *Social interest.* London: Farer and Farer.

Adler, A. (1938). *Social interest: A challenge to mankind.* London: Farer and Farer.

Adler, A. (1956). The individual psychology of Alfred Adler. (H.L. Ansbacher & R. Ansbacher, Eds.). New York: Harper and Row.

Ansbacher, H.L., & Ansbacher, R. (Eds.). (1956). *The individual psychology of Alfred Adler.* New York: Basic Books.

Ansbacher, H.L. (1977). In R. Corsini, *Contemporary personality theories.* Itasca, IL: P.E. Peacock.

Barry, H., & Blane, H.T. (1977). Birth order and alcoholics. *Journal of Individual Psychology*, Vol. 62, pp. 62-79.

Berne, E. (1964). *Games people play.* New York: Grove Press.

Dreikurs, R. (1950). The immediate purpose of children's misbehavior. *International Journal of Individual Psychology*, Vol. 19, pp. 70-87.

Dunlap, K. (1937). *Habits: Their making and unmaking*. New York: Liveright.

Ewen, R.N. (1985). *Introduction to personality theory*, (2nd ed.). New York: Academic Press.

Freud, S. (1900). *The interpretation of dreams*, (A.A. Brill, Ed.), *The basic writings of Sigmund Freud*. Modern Library.

Freud, S. (1920). *Beyond the pleasure principle*. In *Standard Edition*, Vol. 21, London: Hogarth Press.

Freud, S. (1956). *The future of an illusion*. In Standard Edition. Vol. 21, London: Hogarth Press.

Herrill, J.M. (1972). Birth order and the military: A review from the Adlerian perspective. *Journal of Individual Psychology*, Vol. 28, pp. 38-44.

Jones, E. (1955). *The life and work of Sigmund Freud*, (Vol. 2). New York: Basic Books.

Lundin, R.W. (1985). *Theories and systems of psychology* (3rd ed.). Lexington, MA: D.C. Heath.

Mellilo, D. (1983). Birth order, perceived birth order, and family position of academic women. *Journal of Individual Psychology*, Vol. 39, pp. 57-62.

Mosak, H.H. (1973). *Alfred Adler: His influence on psychology today*. Park Ridge, NJ: Noyes Press.

Mosak, H.H. (1979). Adlerian psychotherapy. In R. Corsini (Ed.), *Current psychotherapies*. Itasca, IL: P.E. Peacock.

Orgler, H. (1963). *Alfred Adler: The man and his works*. New York: Capricorn Books.

Pratt, A.B. (1985). Adlerian psychology as an initiative operant system. *The Behavior Analyst*, Vol. 8, pp. 39-51.

Rychman, R.M. (1985). *Theories of personality*, (3rd ed.). Monterey, CA: Brooks Cole Publishers.

Shulman, B.H., & Mosak, H.H. (1988). *Manual for life style assessment*. Muncie, IN: Accelerated Development.

Skinner, B.F. (1938). *The behavior of organisms*. New York: Appleton.

Skinner, B.F. (1953). *Science and human behavior*. New York: Macmillan.

Skinner, B.F. (1971). *Beyond freedom and dignity*. New York: Alfred A. Knopf.

Stark, E. (1985). The sexes. *Psychology Today*, Vol. 19, No. 8, p. 18

Vaihinger, H. (1911). *The philosophy of "as if."* (U.S. Publication, 1925). *New York: Harcourt, Brace and World*.

Way, L. (1942). *Adler's place in psychology*. New York: Collier Books.

INDEX

R

S

ABOUT THE AUTHOR

Robert William Lundin was born in Chicago, Illinois, and spent his early life in the suburb of Highland Park on the shores of Lake Michigan. He received his A.B. degree from DePauw University and his M.A. and Ph.D. degrees in psychology from Indiana University, where he studied under J.R. Kantor and B.F. Skinner. Subsequently, he taught at Denison University and Hamilton College. In 1964 he was appointed Professor of Psychology and Department Chair at The University of the South in Sewanee, Tennessee. In 1982 he was appointed to the William R. Kenan, Jr. Chair at the University. He is a Fellow in the American Psychological Association, a member of the Southeastern Psychological Association and the Society of Sigma Xi.

Books by Lundin include *An Objective Psychology of Music* (first published in 1953, third edition 1985), *Personality: An Experimental Approach* (1961), *Personality: A Behavioral Analysis* (1961, 1974), *Principles of Psychopathology* (1965), *A Study of Behavior* (with George L. Geis and William C. Stebbins, 1965), and *Theories and Systems of Psychology* (1972, 1979, third edition 1985). He has contributed many chapters in edited books on the psychology of music, personality theory, and abnormal behavior.

He has contributed articles to the *Journal of Psychology, Journal of Applied Psychology, Journal of General Psychology, Journal of the History of the Behavioral Sciences, Psychonomic Science* and *The Psychological Record.* He is currently on the editorial board of *The Psychological Record* and is a Licensed Psychologist in the State of Tennessee.